TEACHER'S PET PUBLICATIONS

LITPLAN TEACHER PACK
for
Walk Two Moons
based on the book by
Sharon Creech

Written by
Debra Lemieux

© 2007 Teacher's Pet Publications
All Rights Reserved

This **LitPlan** for
Walk Two Moons
has been brought to you by Teacher's Pet Publications, Inc.

Copyright Teacher's Pet Publications 2007

Only the student materials in this unit plan (such as worksheets, study questions, and tests) may be reproduced multiple times for use in the purchaser's classroom.

For any additional copyright questions,
contact Teacher's Pet Publications.

www.tpet.com

TABLE OF CONTENTS – *Walk Two Moons*

Introduction	5
Unit Objectives	7
Reading Assignment Sheet	8
Unit Outline	9
Study Questions (Short Answer)	13
Quiz/Study Questions (Multiple Choice)	23
Pre-reading Vocabulary Worksheets	45
Lesson One (Introductory Lesson)	67
Oral Reading Evaluation Form	70
Nonfiction Assignment Sheet	84
Writing Assignment 1	73
Writing Assignment 2	89
Writing Assignment 3	95
Writing Evaluation Form	74
Group Project Evaluation Form	87
Vocabulary Review Activities	96
Extra Writing Assignments/Discussion ?s	92
Unit Review Activities	97
Unit Tests	101
Unit Resource Materials	135
Vocabulary Resource Materials	155

A FEW NOTES ABOUT THE AUTHOR
Sharon Creech

Sharon Creech has written numerous books for young adults and was awarded the Newbery Medal for *Walk Two Moons* and the Newbery Honor Award for *The Wanderer*. She has also written *Bloomability, Absolutely Normal Chaos, Chasing Redbird,* and *Pleasing the Ghost*. She was born in South Euclid, Ohio, received a B.A. degree from Hiram College and a M.A. from George Mason University, and has taught high school English in Switzerland and England. She currently resides in the United States. In addition to writing, she enjoys spending time with family, reading, swimming, and kayaking.

INTRODUCTION

This LitPlan has been designed to develop students' reading, writing, thinking, and language skills through exercises and activities related to *Walk Two Moons*. It includes 22 lessons, supported by extra resource materials.

The **introductory lesson** introduces students to the concept of change and how it affects people differently. Following the introductory activity, students are given a transition to explain how the activity relates to the book they are about to read. Following the transition, students are given the materials they will be using during the unit. At the end of the lesson, students begin the pre-reading work for the first reading assignment.

The **reading assignments** are approximately thirty pages each; some are a little shorter while others are a little longer. Students have approximately 15 minutes of pre-reading work to do prior to each reading assignment. This pre-reading work involves reviewing the study questions for the assignment and doing some vocabulary work for 8 to 9 vocabulary words they will encounter in their reading.

The **study guide questions** are fact-based questions; students can find the answers to these questions right in the text. These questions come in two formats: short answer or multiple choice. The best use of these materials is probably to use the short answer version of the questions as study guides for students (since answers will be more complete), and to use the multiple choice version for occasional quizzes.

The **vocabulary work** is intended to enrich students' vocabularies as well as to aid in the students' understanding of the book. Prior to each reading assignment, students will complete a two-part worksheet for approximately 8 to 9 vocabulary words in the upcoming reading assignment. Part I focuses on students' use of general knowledge and contextual clues by giving the sentence in which the word appears in the text. Students are then to write down what they think the words mean based on the words' usage. Part II nails down the definitions of the words by giving students dictionary definitions of the words and having students match the words to the correct definitions based on the words' contextual usage. Students should then have an understanding of the words when they meet them in the text.

After each reading assignment, students will go back and formulate answers for the study guide questions. Discussion of these questions serves as a **review** of the most important events and ideas presented in the reading assignments.

After students complete reading the work, there is a **vocabulary review** lesson which pulls together all of the fragmented vocabulary lists for the reading assignments and gives students a review of all of the words they have studied.

Following the vocabulary review, a lesson is devoted to the **extra discussion questions/writing assignments**. These questions focus on interpretation, critical analysis and personal response, employing a variety of thinking skills and adding to the students' understanding of the novel.

There is a **group theme project** in this unit in which students research one of the national parks or monuments associated with the main character's journey west. They will research the park's history, activities, climate, and most importantly its association with Native Americans.

There are three **writing assignments** in this unit, each with the purpose of informing, persuading, or expressing personal opinions. In the first assignment, students consider the effects of prejudgments on others by writing a persuasive essay to someone who prejudged them. In the second assignment students write to explain the meanings of two poems: "The Tide Rises, The Tide Falls" by Henry Wadsworth Longfellow and "The Horse is NewlY" by e.e. cummings. The third assignment asks students to write their personal opinions regarding what things are important over the course of a lifetime.

There is a **nonfiction reading assignment** that ties in with the group project. Students must read nonfiction magazines, books, etc. to gather information about national parks, monuments, and memorials.

The **review lesson** pulls together all of the aspects of the unit. The teacher is given four or five choices of activities or games to use which all serve the same basic function of reviewing all of the information presented in the unit.

The **unit test** comes in two formats: multiple choice or short answer. As a convenience, two different tests for each format have been included. There is also an advanced short answer unit test for advanced students.

There are additional **support materials** included with this unit. The **Unit Resource Materials** section includes suggestions for an in-class library, crossword and word search puzzles related to the novel, and extra worksheets. There is a list of **bulletin board ideas** which gives the teacher suggestions for bulletin boards to go along with this unit. In addition, there is a list of **extra class activities** the teacher could choose from to enhance the unit or as a substitution for an exercise the teacher might feel is inappropriate for his/her class. **Answer keys** are located directly after the **reproducible student materials** throughout the unit. The **Vocabulary Resource Materials** section includes similar worksheets and games to reinforce the vocabulary words.

The **level** of this unit can be varied depending upon the criteria on which the individual assignments are graded, the teacher's expectations of his/her students in class discussions, and the formats chosen for the study guides, quizzes and test. If teachers have other ideas/activities they wish to use, they can usually easily be inserted prior to the review lesson.

The student materials may be reproduced for use in the teacher's classroom without infringement of copyrights. No other portion of this unit may be reproduced without the written consent of Teacher's Pet Publications, Inc.

UNIT OBJECTIVES – *Walk Two Moons*

1. Through reading Marion Creech's *Walk Two Moons*, students will consider the concept of change and how it affects people differently.

2. Students will demonstrate their understanding of the text on four levels: factual, interpretive, critical and personal.

3. Students will reflect upon the effects of prejudgments.

4. Students will be given the opportunity to practice reading aloud and silently to improve their skills in each area.

5. Students will answer questions to demonstrate their knowledge and understanding of the main events and characters in *Walk Two Moons* as they relate to the author's theme development.

6. Students will enrich their vocabularies and improve their understanding of the novel through the vocabulary lessons prepared for use in conjunction with the novel.

7. The writing assignments in this unit are geared to several purposes:
    a. To have students demonstrate their abilities to inform, to persuade, or to express their own personal ideas
        Note: Students will demonstrate ability to write effectively to <u>inform</u> by developing and organizing facts to convey information. Students will demonstrate the ability to write effectively to <u>persuade</u> by selecting and organizing relevant information, establishing an argumentative purpose, and by designing an appropriate strategy for an identified audience. Students will demonstrate the ability to write effectively to <u>express personal ideas</u> by selecting a form and its appropriate elements.
    b. To check the students' reading comprehension
    c. To make students think about the ideas presented by the novel
    d. To encourage logical thinking
    e. To provide an opportunity to practice good grammar and improve students' use of the English language.

8. Students will read aloud, report, and participate in large and small group discussions to improve their public speaking and personal interaction skills.

READING ASSIGNMENT SHEET – *Walk Two Moons*

Date Assigned	Chapters Assigned	Completion Date
	1-5	
	6-10	
	11-14	
	15-19	
	20-23	
	24-28	
	29-32	
	33-39	
	40-44	

UNIT OUTLINE – *Walk Two Moons*

1 Introduction	2 PVR Ch 1-5	3 ?s 1-5 PVR Ch 6-10	4 ?s 6-10 PV 11-14 Writing #1	5 ?s Vocab R 11-14 Writing #1
6 ?s 11-14 PVR 15-19	7 ?s 15-19 Quiz 1-19 Writing Styles	8 Intro Group Project PVR 20-23	9 ?s 20-23 PVR 24-28	10 ?s 42-28 Group Project
11 PVR 29-32 Group Project	12 ?s 29-32 Writing #2	13 PVR 33-39 Writing #2	14 ?s 33-39 Group Project	15 PVR 40-44 Group Project
16 ?s 40-44 Extra Discussion ?s	17 Extra Discussion ?s	18 Group Project Presentations	19 Writing #3	20 Vocab Review
21 Unit Review	22 Unit Test			

Key: P = Preview Study Questions V = Vocabulary Work R= Read

STUDY GUIDE QUESTIONS

SHORT ANSWER STUDY QUESTIONS
Walk Two Moons

Chapters 1-5
1. Whose face did Sal see "pressed up against an upstairs window next door"?
2. Who was Sal locked in a car with for six days?
3. What did Sal's father do when he learned Sal's mother was not returning home?
4. Where did Sal and her grandparents go on their trip?
5. Once Sal decided to go on the trip, she prayed she would be in Idaho by when?
6. What was Sal's real name and for what was she named?
7. In the car, Sal entertained her grandparents with stories about whom?
8. Who was Mrs. Partridge?
9. Give an example of how Sal's grandparents got into trouble.

Chapters 6-10
1. Why did Mr. and Mrs. Winterbottom remind Sal of her other grandparents, the Pickfords?
2. What did Phoebe think about Mrs. Cadaver?
3. Into what body of water did Gram put her feet?
4. What whispering words did Sal hear on the way to Idaho?
5. Who rang Phoebe's doorbell one Saturday morning when Phoebe's parents were out?
6. When Sal first visited Mary Lou Finney's house, what were Mr. and Mrs. Finney doing?
7. Who drew a picture of Sal as a lizard-like creature with long black hair?
8. What secret did Mrs. Winterbottom want to keep from Mr. Winterbottom?
9. What mysterious message was left in an envelope on Phoebe's front step?
10. What did Sal find Gram doing at "The Wisconsin Dells"?

Chapters 11-14
1. Another message was left on Phoebe's front steps. What did this message say?
2. Which term did Sal's mother and Gram not like?
3. How was Pipestone, Minnesota similar to Bybanks, Kentucky?
4. Why did Gramps purchase Sal a peace pipe?
5. When Gramps asked Gram to marry him, what did Gram say?
6. Who was Mr. Birkway?
7. "We had absolutely no idea all the trouble they were going to cause." To what did this statement refer?
8. What did Phoebe *not* notice about her mother?
9. What did Sal's father want to tell her?

Walk Two Moons Short Answer Study Questions page 2

Chapters 15-19
1. What happened to Gram while she was wading in the Missouri River?
2. Who was Tom Fleet?
3. From what type of tree did Sal hear the beautiful birdsong coming?
4. About what important thing was Prudence worried?
5. How did Sal describe her father?
6. Sal's mother said she had to leave in order to do what?
7. Sal's mother left Sal a good-bye letter. In the letter, when did she say she would return?
8. How did Phoebe respond when she encountered "the lunatic"?

Chapters 20-23
1. What did Sal write about in her journal for Mr. Birkway?
2. How did Ben get to hold hands with Sal?
3. What did Mrs. Winterbottom's note to Mr. Winterbottom say?
4. Phoebe told her classmates that her mother was away in what city?
5. What did Phoebe think happened to her mother?
6. Why was Gramps worried about Gram?
7. Sal continued to hear whispers in the air. What were they saying?
8. Who found Sal after she fell from an oak tree?
9. What happened the night Sal fell from the oak tree?

Chapters 24-28
1. What did Phoebe eat for dinner at the Finneys'?
2. Who did Phoebe quote when she said, "In life, you have to make some sacrifices"?
3. Who heard Phoebe crying?
4. What decision did Phoebe make regarding her mother?
5. According to Phoebe's oral report, what did "Pandora" mean?
6. What was the only good thing in Pandora's box?
7. When "everything seems fine and good," what did Sal do?
8. To whom were The Black Hills sacred?
9. How did Sal react to Mt. Rushmore?

Chapters 29-32
1. Who said, "Maybe dying should be normal and terrible"?
2. After Phoebe shared the story of her mother's disappearance with Sergeant Bickle, he excused himself and returned with whom?
3. Why did Sal like Phoebe?
4. What did Sal find unsettling about Mrs. Partridge?
5. What did Mr. Birkway share with the class?
6. Who did Sal recognize in Sergeant Bickle's photograph?
7. What did Sal find out about Mr. Birkway?
8. What made Mr. Birkway regret sharing the journals?

Walk Two Moons Short Answer Study Questions page 3

Chapters 33-39
1. How did Mrs. Cadaver's husband die?
2. What was Gram waiting her entire life to see?
3. Who did Phoebe and Sal plan to find?
4. What was the lunatic's name?
5. Who did Sal see holding hands and kissing?
6. Why did Ben's mother remind Sal of her own mother?
7. When Mrs. Winterbottom returned home, what was different about her?
8. What was the second reason Phoebe almost fainted?
9. What was Mrs. Winterbottom scared to tell her husband?

Chapters 40-44
1. Who had been leaving the messages on Phoebe's porch?
2. What did Ben give Sal?
3. When Sal and her grandparents arrived in Coeur D'Alene, where did they go?
4. What did it take Sal four hours to do?
5. What did Sal want to "scour every inch of"?
6. Where did the sheriff take Sal?
7. Who survived the bus crash?
8. When Sal said, "This ain't your marriage bed," how did Gramps reply?"
9. What did Gramps name his new beagle puppy?
10. What was the third thing Sal was jealous of?

ANSWER KEY SHORT ANSWER STUDY GUIDE QUESTIONS – *Walk Two Moons*

Chapters 1-5

1. Whose face did Sal see "pressed up against an upstairs window next door"?
   She saw the face of Phoebe Winterbottom, a girl who would become Sal's friend.

2. Who was Sal locked in a car with for six days?
   She was locked in a car with her grandparents.

3. What did Sal's father do when he learned Sal's mother was not returning home?
   He pounded on the living room plaster wall with a chisel and a hammer and uncovered a brick fireplace.

4. Where did Sal and her grandparents go on their trip?
   They drove two thousand miles west to Lewiston, Idaho.

5. Once Sal decided to go on the trip, she prayed she would be in Idaho by when?
   She prayed to get to Idaho by her mother's birthday.

6. What was Sal's real name and for what was she named?
   Sal's real name was Salamanca Tree Hiddle. Her parents named her Salamanca because they mistakenly thought it was the name of her great-great grandmother's Indian tribe. Sal's middle name, Tree, came from her mother's love of trees.

7. In the car, Sal entertained her grandparents with stories about whom?
   She told tales about Phoebe Winterbottom.

8. Who was Mrs. Partridge?
   Mrs. Partridge was Margaret Cadaver's mother.

9. Give an example of how Sal's grandparents got into trouble.
   In Washington D.C., they were arrested for stealing the back tires off a senator's car. Actually, they were only borrowing the tires because their own had gone flat.
   In Philadelphia, police stopped them for driving on the shoulder of the road.

Chapters 6-10

1. Why did Mr. and Mrs. Winterbottom remind Sal of her other grandparents, the Pickfords?
   They spoke quietly, sat up straight when they ate their food, and were polite to each other.

2. What did Phoebe think about Mrs. Cadaver?
   Phoebe thought Mrs. Cadaver killed Mr. Cadaver, chopped him up, and buried him in the backyard.

3. Into what body of water did Gram put her feet?
   She put her feet into Lake Michigan.

4. What whispering words did Sal hear on the way to Idaho?
   The words were, "Rush, hurry, rush."

5. Who rang Phoebe's doorbell one Saturday morning when Phoebe's parents were out?
   A nervous, young man who appeared to be about seventeen or eighteen rang the bell.

6. When Sal first visited Mary Lou Finney's house, what were Mr. and Mrs. Finney doing?
   Mr. Finney was lying in the bathtub with his clothes on, reading a book. Mrs. Finney was lying on top of the garage with a pillow under her head.

7. Who drew a picture of Sal as a lizard-like creature with long black hair?
   Ben Finney drew that picture.

8. What secret did Mrs. Winterbottom want to keep from Mr. Winterbottom?
   She did not want to tell him about the boy who stopped by the house.

9. What mysterious message was left in an envelope on Phoebe's front step?
   "Don't judge a man until you've walked two moons in his moccasins."

10. What did Sal find Gram doing at "The Wisconsin Dells"?
    She was dancing with the Indians.

Chapters 11-14
1. Another message was left on Phoebe's front steps. What did this message say?
   It said, "Everyone has his own agenda."

2. Which term did Sal's mother and Gram not like?
   They didn't like the name "Native American."

3. How was Pipestone, Minnesota similar to Bybanks, Kentucky?
   The air smelled the same. People talked to each other and would say hello when they passed by.

4. Why did Gramps purchase Sal a peace pipe?
   He told Sal, "It's for remembering with."

5. When Gramps asked Gram to marry him, what did Gram say?
   She said, "Do you have a dog?"

6. Who was Mr. Birkway?
   Mr. Birkway was Sal's teacher.

7. "We had absolutely no idea all the trouble they were going to cause." To what did this statement refer?
   This statement referred to the journals Mr. Birkway collected.

8. What did Phoebe *not* notice about her mother?
   Phoebe did not notice that her mother had been crying and that she was worried about something.

9. What did Sal's father want to tell her?
   He wanted to tell Sal something about Margaret Cadaver.

Chapters 15-19

1. What happened to Gram while she was wading in the Missouri River?
   A water moccasin bit her.

2. Who was Tom Fleet?
   He was a boy who initially threatened Sal and her grandparents but who helped save Gram's life.

3. From what type of tree did Sal hear the beautiful birdsong coming?
   She heard it coming from an aspen tree.

4. About what important thing was Prudence worried?
   She was worried about cheerleading tryouts.

5. How did Sal describe her father?
   She described him as "a kind, honest, simple, and good man." She explained that she meant *simple* as in "he likes plain and simple things" – not as in "simple-minded."

6. Sal's mother said she had to leave in order to do what?
   She wanted to clear her head and "to clear her heart of all the bad things." She also wanted to learn about what she was on her own.

7. Sal's mother left Sal a good-bye letter. In the letter, when did she say she would return?
   She said she would return before the tulips bloom.

8. How did Phoebe respond when she encountered "the lunatic"?
   She pushed him, yanked Sal's arm, and ran home. Once inside the house, Phoebe told her mother to either call the police or her father, but Mrs. Winterbottom did neither.

Chapters 20-23
1. What did Sal write about in her journal for Mr. Birkway?
   She wrote about the blackberry kiss, a memory associated with her mother.

2. How did Ben get to hold hands with Sal?
   He asked if she wanted her palm read.

3. What did Mrs. Winterbottom's note to Mr. Winterbottom say?
   "I had to go away. I can't explain. I'll call you in a few days."

4. Phoebe told her classmates that her mother was away in what city?
   She told them her mother was away in London.

5. What did Phoebe think happened to her mother?
   Phoebe believed the lunatic kidnaped her mother.

6. Why was Gramps worried about Gram?
   Gramps was worried about Gram's raspy breathing.

7. Sal continued to hear whispers in the air. What were they saying?
   They said, "Slow down, slow, slow, slow."

8. Who found Sal after she fell from an oak tree?
   Her mother found her.

9. What happened the night Sal fell from the tree?
   Sal's mother gave birth, but the baby was stillborn.

Chapters 24-28
1. What did Phoebe eat for dinner at the Finneys'?
   She ate dried-up muesli without milk.

2. Who did Phoebe quote when she said, "In life, you have to make some sacrifices?"
   Phoebe quoted her mother.

3. Who heard Phoebe crying?
   Sal's father heard her.

4. What decision did Phoebe make regarding her mother?
   She decided to call the police.

5. According to Phoebe's oral report, what did "Pandora" mean?
   It meant "the gift of all."

6. What was the only good thing in Pandora's box?
   Hope was the only good thing.

7. When "everything seems fine and good," what did Sal do?
   She worried that something will go wrong and change everything.

8. To whom were The Black Hills sacred?
   They were sacred to the Sioux Indians.

9. How did Sal react to Mt. Rushmore?
   She thought the carving of the Presidents' faces into the Siouxs' sacred hill must have made them sad.

Chapters 29-32
1. Who said, "Maybe dying should be normal and terrible."
   Ben said, "Maybe dying should be normal and terrible."

2. After Phoebe shared the story of her mother's disappearance witho Sergeant Bickle, he excused himself and returned with whom?
   He returned with Mr. Winterbottom.

3. Why did Sal like Phoebe?
   In spite of Phoebe's annoying ways, Sal liked Phoebe and was drawn to her. Sal felt that Phoebe "acted out the way I sometimes felt."

4. What did Sal find unsettling about Mrs. Partridge?
   Despite being blind, Mrs. Partridge could see everything Phoebe was doing.

5. What did Mr. Birkway share with the class?
   He shared passages from the students' journals.

6. Who did Sal recognize in Sergeant Bickle's photograph?
   She recognized the lunatic.

7. What did Sal find out about Mr. Birkway?
   She learned he was Mrs. Partridge's son and Mrs. Cadaver's twin brother.

8. What made Mr. Birkway regret sharing the journals?
   He read a passage which suggested his sister, Mrs. Cadaver, was a murderer.

Chapters 33-39
1. How did Mrs. Cadaver's husband die?
    A drunk driver rammed into his car.

2. What was Gram waiting her entire life to see?
    She was waiting to see Old Faithful.

3. Who did Phoebe and Sal plan to find?
    They were going to find both Sergeant Bickle's son and Phoebe's mother.

4. What was the lunatic's name?
    His name was Mike.

5. Who did Sal see holding hands and kissing?
    She saw Mrs. Winterbottom and the lunatic holding hands and kissing.

6. Why did Ben's mother remind Sal of her own mother?
    Ben's mother wandered aimlessly across the hospital lawn, much like Sal's mother did when she returned from the hospital.

7. When Mrs. Winterbottom returned home, what was different about her?
    Her hair was short and stylish, and she had on makeup. She was also wearing jeans and a T – shirt.

8. What was the second reason Phoebe almost fainted?
    Mike Bickle (the lunatic) was in her living room.

9. What was Mrs. Winterbottom scared to tell her husband?
    She was scared to tell him that Mike Bickle was her son.

Chapters 40-44
1. Who had been leaving the messages on Phoebe's porch?
    Mrs. Partridge had been leaving the messages.

2. What did Ben give Sal?
    Ben gave Sal a chicken.

3. When Sal and her grandparents arrived in Coeur D'Alene, where did they go?
    They went to the hospital.

4. What did it take Sal four hours to do?
    It took her four hours to drive one hundred miles to the top of Lewiston Hill.

5. What did Sal want to "scour every inch of"?
   She wanted to scour the inside of the bus that skidded off the road and down the hill. She was looking for something familiar inside the bus.

6. Where did the sheriff take Sal?
   He took Sal to her mother's grave.

7. Who survived the bus crash?
   Mrs. Cadaver survived the crash.

8. When Sal said, "This ain't your marriage bed," how did Gramps reply?"
   Gramps replied, "But it will have to do."

9. What did Gramps name his new beagle puppy?
   He named the puppy "Huzza Huzza."

10. What was the third thing Sal was jealous of?
    She was jealous that Phoebe's mother came back while her own mother did not.

STUDY GUIDE/QUIZ QUESTIONS – *Walk Two Moons*
Multiple Choice Format

Chapters 1-5

1. Whose face did Sal see "pressed up against an upstairs window next door"?
    a. She saw the face of Margaret Cadaver, her father's new friend.
    b. She saw her grandmother's face.
    c. She saw the face of Phoebe Winterbottom, a girl who would become Sal's friend.
    d. She saw her classmate, Mary Lou Finney.

2. Who was Sal locked in a car with for six days?
    a. Phoebe Winterbottom
    b. Her grandparents
    c. Her father
    d. Margaret Cadaver

3. What did Sal's father do when he learned Sal's mother was not returning home?
    a. He quit his job and moved in with his parents.
    b. He pounded on the living room plaster wall with a chisel and a hammer and uncovered a brick fireplace.
    c. He moved to Idaho where he found a job selling agricultural projects.
    d. He drove to Idaho to persuade her to return home.

4. Where did Sal and her grandparents go on their trip?
    a. They drove four hours to Philadelphia to visit Sal's cousins.
    b. They drove to Washington D.C. to tour museums and monuments.
    c. They drove to Kentucky where Sal lived for most of her thirteen years.
    d. They drove two thousand miles west to Lewiston, Idaho.

5. Once Sal decided to go on the trip, she prayed she would be in Idaho by when?
    a. She prayed she would be in Idaho before it started to snow.
    b. She prayed she would be in Idaho before the start of the school year.
    c. She prayed she would be in Idaho by her mother's birthday.
    d. She prayed she would be in Idaho before she turned fourteen.

6. What was Sal's real name?
    a. Salamanca Tree Hiddle
    b. Chickabiddy Hiddle
    c. Sally Pickford
    d. Sal Chanhassen Pickford

Walk Two Moons Multiple Choice Study/Quiz Questions Chapters 1-5 (continued)

7. In the car, Sal entertained her grandparents with stories about whom?
    a. Phoebe Winterbottom
    b. Her mother and father
    c. Her math teacher
    d. Margaret Cadaver

8. Who was Mrs. Partridge?
    a. Sal's teacher
    b. Sal's aunt
    c. Phoebe Winterbottom's grandmother
    d. Margaret Cadaver's mother

9. Which is an example of how Sal's grandparents got into trouble?
    a. At the airport, they got into trouble for failing to show proper identification.
    b. In Washington D.C., they were arrested for stealing the back tires off a senator's car.
    c. In Philadelphia, they got into trouble for touching famous works of art.
    d. They got into trouble for bringing their pets into a restaurant.

Walk Two Moons Multiple Choice Study/Quiz Questions

Chapters 6-10
1. Why did Mr. and Mrs. Winterbottom remind Sal of her other grandparents, the Pickfords?
    a. They had an accent when they spoke.
    b. They wore the same style of old-fashioned clothes and drove the same car.
    c. They liked the outdoors and traveled to national parks in the summer.
    d. They spoke quietly, sat up straight when they eat their food, and were polite to each other.

2. What did Phoebe think about Mrs. Cadaver?
    a. Phoebe thought Mrs. Cadaver killed Mr. Cadaver, chopped him up, and buried him in the backyard.
    b. Phoebe thought Mrs. Cadaver stole jewelry from Mrs. Finney.
    c. Phoebe thought Mrs. Cadaver was a noisy neighbor who spied on people in the neighborhood.
    d. Phoebe thought Mrs. Cadaver was a famous artist who moved to the neighborhood for privacy.

3. Into what body of water did Gram put her feet?
    a. Lake Huron
    b. The Atlantic Ocean
    c. The Mississippi River
    d. Lake Michigan

4. What whispering words did Sal hear on the way to Idaho?
    a. "Be careful, don't get hurt."
    b. "Rush, hurry, rush."
    c. "Remember, I love you."
    d. "Don't worry. You'll find out the truth."

5. Who rang Phoebe's doorbell one Saturday morning when Phoebe's parents were out?
    a. Margaret Cadaver who was looking for her lost cat
    b. Mary Lou Finney who was trying to figure out her weekend homework assignment
    c. A nervous, young man of about seventeen or eighteen
    d. A mysterious woman asking for directions to Cleveland

alk Two Moons Multiple Choice Study/Quiz Questions Chapters 6-10 (continued)

6. When Sal first visited Mary Lou Finney's house, what were Mr. and Mrs. Finney doing?
    a. Mrs. Finney was baking an apple pie. Mr. Finney was reading the sports section of the newspaper.
    b. Mr. Finney, fully-clothed, was lying in the bathtub reading a book. Mrs. Finney was lying on top of the garage with a pillow under her head.
    c. Mr. Finney was playing football with Mary Lou's brothers, and Mrs. Finney was helping Mary Lou with her homework.
    d. Mrs. Finney was arm-wrestling with the boys. Mr. Finney was watching his favorite soap opera.

7. Who drew a picture of Sal as a lizard-like creature with long black hair?
    a. Ben Finney
    b. Phoebe
    c. Mary Lou Finney
    d. The boy that sits next to her in school

8. What secret did Mrs. Winterbottom want to keep from Mr. Winterbottom?
    a. She did not want to tell him she lost her job at Rocky's Rubber.
    b. She did not want to tell him about the fight between Phoebe and Prudence.
    c. She did not want to tell him about the money she found at the park.
    d. She did not want to tell him about the boy who stopped by the house.

9. What mysterious message was left in an envelope on Phoebe's front step?
    a. "Don't judge a man until you've walked two moons in his moccasins."
    b. "Cadaver means dead body."
    c. "Don't make a mountain out of a mole hill."
    d. "Always lock your doors and windows."

10. What did Sal find Gram going at "The Wisconsin Dells"?
    a. She was reading a trail map because she is lost.
    b. She was taking a nap under a maple tree.
    c. She was taking photos of Lakes Mendota and Monona.
    d. She was dancing with the Indians.

Walk Two Moons Multiple Choice Study/Quiz Questions

<u>Chapters 11-14</u>

1. Another message was left on Phoebe's front steps. What did this message say?
    a. "Be as gentle as a lamb."
    b. "Everyone has his own agenda."
    c. "Don't bite off more than you can chew."
    d. "Time flies."

2. Which term did Sal's mother and Gram not like?
    a. Native American
    b. Peace Pipe
    c. Injun Joe
    d. Indian Joe

3. How was Pipestone, Minnesota similar to Bybanks, Kentucky?
    a. The houses and the town hall were alike.
    b. Both places had gentle rolling hills and scenic crystal-clear lakes.
    c. Each place had a covered bridge and lots of tall aspen trees.
    d. The air smelled the same. People talked to each other and would say hello when they passed by.

4. Why did Gramps purchase Sal a peace pipe?
    a. He wanted Sal to give it to her father.
    b. Gramps believed it would keep Sal safe.
    c. He wanted Sal to keep it for him.
    d. He told her, "It's for remembering with."

5. When Gramps asked Gram to marry him, what did Gram say?
    a. "Do you have a dog?"
    b. "How old are you?"
    c. "Do you want a family?"
    d. "What is your real name?"

6. Who was Mr. Birkway?
    a. Sal's physician
    b. Sal's teacher
    c. Gramps's best friend
    d. Phoebe's uncle

Walk Two Moons Multiple Choice Study/Quiz Questions Chapters 11-14 (continued)

7. "We had absolutely no idea all the trouble they were going to cause." To what did this statement refer?
    a. The peace pipes Gramps purchased.
    b. The cartoons Ben drew.
    c. The journals Mr. Birkway collected.
    d. The articles in the newspaper about Mrs. Cadaver.

8. What did Phoebe *not* notice about her mother?
    a. Phoebe did not notice that her mother had been crying and that she was worried about something.
    b. Phoebe did not notice that her mother dyed her hair red.
    c. Phoebe did not notice that her mother has stopped cooking healthy food.
    d. Phoebe did not notice that her mother had been rushing around the house to hide something.

9. What did Sal's father want to tell her?
    a. He wanted to tell Sal he loved her.
    b. He wanted to tell Sal a secret about her mother.
    c. He wanted to tell Sal something about Margaret Cadaver.
    d. He wanted to tell Sal that they were moving soon.

Walk Two Moons Multiple Choice Study/Quiz Questions

<u>Chapters 15-19</u>
1. What happened to Gram while she was wading in the Missouri River?
    a. She tripped on a rock and cut her knee.
    b. She found an old bottle floating in the water with a message inside.
    c. She dropped her purse in the water, and it floated away from her.
    d. A water moccasin bit her.

2. Who was Tom Fleet?
    a. Mr. Hiddle's best friend
    b. A man who wanted to meet Phoebe because he claimed to know the lunatic
    c. A boy who initially threatened Sal and her grandparents but who helped save Gram's life
    d. Mrs. Cadaver's nightshift co-worker

3. From what type of tree did Sal hear the beautiful birdsong coming?
    a. An aspen tree
    b. A sugar maple tree
    c. An oak tree
    d. A palm tree

4. What important thing was Prudence worried about?
    a. She was worried about her geometry test.
    b. She was worried about her mother's change in behavior.
    c. She was worried about cheerleading tryouts.
    d. She was worried about Phoebe's encounter with the lunatic.

5. How did Sal describe her father?
    a. She described him as a "hard working and smart man."
    b. She described him as a "preoccupied and busy man."
    c. She described him as an "athletic, active, and healthy man."
    d. She described him as "a kind, honest, simple, and good man."

6. Sal's mother said she had to leave in order to do what?
    a. She wanted to get away from Bybanks and "see the world."
    b. She wanted to "find happiness by being an inspiration to others."
    c. She wanted to clear her head and "to clear her heart of all the bad things."
    d. She wanted to "restore the shattered relationship with her parents and siblings."

Walk Two Moons Multiple Choice Study/Quiz Questions Chapters 15-19 (continued)

7. Sal's mother left Sal a good-bye letter. In the letter, when did she say she would return?
    a. Before the snow falls
    b. Before the tulips bloom
    c. Before Sal's birthday
    d. Before summer vacation

8. How did Phoebe respond when she encountered "the lunatic"?
    a. She screamed and punched him in the eye.
    b. She pushed him, yanked Sal's arm, and ran home.
    c. She called him a crazy lunatic and told him to leave her alone.
    d. She begged him to explain why he kept following her.

Walk Two Moons Multiple Choice Study/Quiz Questions

<u>Chapters 20-23</u>
1. What did Sal write about in her journal for Mr. Birkway?
    a. Her beloved pet rabbit
    b. An Indian story about the passing of the seasons
    c. The sad journey to Euclid, Ohio
    d. The blackberry kiss–a memory associated with her mother

2. How did Ben get to hold hands with Sal?
    a. He asked if she wanted her palm read.
    b. He handed her some change.
    c. He shook her hand but did not let go.
    d. He told her she was too tense.

3. What did Mrs. Winterbottom's note to Mr. Winterbottom say?
    a. "Don't forget to take out the trash and empty the dishwasher."
    b. "I had to go away. I can't explain. I'll call you in a few days."
    c. "Please forgive me, but my agenda is different than yours."
    d. "Don't judge me. Everything will make sense in a few weeks."

4. Phoebe told her classmates that her mother was away in what city?
    a. Tokyo
    b. London
    c. Chicago
    d. Paris

5. What did Phoebe think happened to her mother?
    a. Phoebe believed the lunatic kidnaped her mother.
    b. Phoebe thought her mother was somewhere with Mrs. Cadaver.
    c. Phoebe believed her mother left to start a new life in London.
    d. Phoebe thought her mother ran away with Sal's mother.

6. Why was Gramps worried about Gram?
    a. Gramps thought she was forgetting too many things.
    b. Gramps was worried about her insomnia and physical weakness.
    c. Gramps thought Gram was going to leave him for an old boyfriend.
    d. Gramps was worried about Gram's raspy breathing.

7. Sal continued to hear whispers in the air. What were they saying?
    a. "Be alert, don't get hurt."
    b. "You're almost there."
    c. "Remember, I love you."
    d. "Slow down, slow, slow, slow."

Walk Two Moons Multiple Choice Study/Quiz Questions Chapters 20-23 (continued)

8. Who found Sal after she fell from an oak tree?
   a. Her mother
   b. Her father
   c. Gramps
   d. Gram

9. What happened the night Sal fell from the tree?
   a. Her mother decided to leave.
   b. Sal learned the truth about her grandparents.
   c. Sal's mother gave birth, but the baby was stillborn.
   d. Sal told her parents about the mysterious stranger.

Walk Two Moons Multiple Choice Study/Quiz Questions

Chapters 24-28
1. What did Phoebe eat for dinner at the Finneys'?
    a. Dried-up muesli without milk
    b. Fried chicken and beans
    c. Vegetarian spaghetti with red bean salad
    d. Brownies

2. Who did Phoebe quote when she said, "In life, you have to make some sacrifices"?
    a. Phoebe quoted her father.
    b. Phoebe quoted Sal.
    c. Phoebe quoted her sister.
    d. Phoebe quoted her mother.

3. Who heard Phoebe crying?
    a. Sal's father
    b. Phoebe's father
    c. Prudence
    d. Ben

4. What decision did Phoebe make regarding her mother?
    a. She decided to search for her mother.
    b. She decided to call the police.
    c. She decided to telephone all her mother's friends.
    d. She decided to confront the lunatic.

5. According to Phoebe's oral report, what did "Pandora" mean?
    a. Fire
    b. The gift of all
    c. Lover of beauty
    d. Plentiful

6. What was the only good thing in Pandora's box?
    a. Love
    b. Friendship
    c. Hope
    d. Family

7. When "everything seemed fine and good," what did Sal do?
    a. She daydreamed about family memories.
    b. She went for a walk to appreciate nature's beauty.
    c. She listened for the birdsong.
    d. She worried that something would go wrong and change everything.

Walk Two Moons Multiple Choice Study/Quiz Questions Chapters 24-28 (continued)

8. To whom were the Black Hills sacred?
    a. The Sioux Indians
    b. The Cherokee Indians
    c. The Blackfoot Indians
    d. The Seminole Indians

9. How did Sal react to Mt. Rushmore?
    a. She imagined the face of her mother carved alongside the Presidents' faces.
    b. She thought it was the most beautiful attraction in North America.
    c. She thought the carving of the Presidents' faces into the Sioux's sacred hill must have made them sad.
    d. She wondered what the faces would look like in the twilight hours and wished she could remain for the evening illumination.

Walk Two Moons Multiple Choice Study/Quiz Questions

<u>Chapters 29-32</u>
1. Who said, "Maybe dying should be normal and terrible."
    a. Ben
    b. Sal
    c. Mr. Hiddle
    d. Gram

2. After Phoebe shared the story of her mother's disappearance with Sergeant Bickle, he excused himself and returned with whom?
    a. Mrs. Winterbottom
    b. Mrs. Cadaver
    c. A police detective
    d. Mr. Winterbottom

3. Why did Sal like Phoebe?
    a. Sal felt that Phoebe "acted out the way I sometimes felt."
    b. Sal liked Phoebe's ability "to tell the truth no matter the cost."
    c. Sal felt that Phoebe was like "the sister she never had."
    d. Sal liked Phoebe's "dramatic tendencies."

4. What did Sal find unsettling about Mrs. Partridge?
    a. Sal found it unsettling that Mrs. Partridge lived with Margaret Cadaver.
    b. Despite being blind, Mrs. Partridge could see everything Phoebe was doing.
    c. Mrs. Partridge was always reading a mystery book.
    d. Sal found it unsettling that Mrs. Partridge never seemed to sleep.

5. What did Mr. Birkway share with the class?
    a. He shared left-over candy from Halloween.
    b. He shared memories of his days in college.
    c. He shared letters from previous students.
    d. He shared passages from the students' journals.

6. Who did Sal recognize in Sergeant Bickle's photograph?
    a. Ben
    b. Mrs. Winterbottom
    c. Mrs. Bickle
    d. The lunatic

Walk Two Moons Multiple Choice Study/Quiz Questions Chapters 29-32 (continued)

7. What did Sal find out about Mr. Birkway?
    a. She learned he was her mother's former boyfriend.
    b. She learned he was Mrs. Partridge's son and Mrs. Cadaver's twin brother.
    c. She learned he worked as a waiter on the weekends.
    d. She learned he knew the lunatic.

8. What made Mr. Birkway regret sharing the journals?
    a. He finally realized that it was harming relationships among his students.
    b. When he lost one of the journals, a student found it and shared it with everyone.
    c. He read a passage which suggested his sister, Mrs. Cadaver, was a murderer.
    d. He realizes reading the journals aloud is not teaching his students how to write.

Walk Two Moons Multiple Choice Study/Quiz Questions

Chapters 33-39
1. How did Mrs. Cadaver's husband die?
   a. He had a heart attack.
   b. He fell off a tractor.
   c. He was shot in a hunting accident.
   d. A drunk driver rammed into his car.

2. What had Gram been waiting her entire life to see?
   a. Mt. Rushmore
   b. Old Faithful
   c. The Aztec Ruins
   d. The giant sequoias

3. Who did Phoebe and Sal plan to find?
   a. They were going to persuade Sal's father to help them locate Phoebe's mother.
   b. They were going to find the lunatic.
   c. They were going to find both Sergeant Bickle's son and Phoebe's mother.
   d. They were going to find Mr. Birkway's mother.

4. What was the lunatic's name?
   a. Joe
   b. Dave
   c. Mike
   d. Tommy

5. Who did Sal see holding hands and kissing?
   a. Sergeant Bickle and Mrs. Winterbottom
   b. Mrs. Winterbottom and the lunatic
   c. Ben and Mary Lou
   d. Margaret Cadaver and her father

6. Why did Ben's mother remind Sal of her own mother?
   a. Ben's mother had long, black hair and a thoughtful personality, just like Sal's mother.
   b. Ben's mother wandered aimlessly, much like Sal's mother did when she returned from the hospital.
   c. They both loved nature, reading, and their families.
   d. Both had made tremendous sacrifices for their families.

Walk Two Moons Multiple Choice Study/Quiz Questions Chapters 33-39 (continued)

7. When Mrs. Winterbottom returned home, what is different about her?
   a. Her hair was short and stylish, and she had on makeup.
   b. She was tired and appeared to have lost weight.
   c. She was less willing to do everything for her children and husband.
   d. She had quit her old job and enrolled in college to become a lawyer.

8. What was the second reason Phoebe almost fainted?
   a. Sergeant Bickle arrested her mother.
   b. Mr. Winterbottom said he was leaving for good.
   c. Her mother refused to return back home.
   d. Mike Bickle (the lunatic) was in Phoebe's living room.

9. What was Mrs. Winterbottom scared to tell her husband?
   a. She was scared to tell him that she was arrested.
   b. She was scared to tell him she did not love him any more.
   c. She was scared to tell him the truth about the messages.
   d. She was scared to tell him that Mike Bickle was her son.

Walk Two Moons Multiple Choice Study/Quiz Questions

Chapters 40-44
1. Who had been leaving the messages on Phoebe's porch?
   a. Mrs. Partridge
   b. Phoebe
   c. Mike (the lunatic)
   d. Mrs. Cadaver

2. What did Ben give Sal?
   a. A ring
   b. A puppy
   c. A tree
   d. A chicken

3. When Sal and her grandparents arrived in Coeur D'Alene, where did they go?
   a. They went on a tour of the lake.
   b. They went to the sheriff's office.
   c. They went to the hospital.
   d. They went to a motel.

4. What did it take Sal four hours to do?
   a. It took her four hours to learn how to drive a car.
   b. It took her four hours to convince Gramps to drive back to Ohio.
   c. It took her four hours to drive one hundred miles to the top of Lewiston Hill.
   d. It took her four hours to work up the courage to leave Coeur D'Alene.

5. What did Sal want to "scour every inch of"?
   a. She wanted to scour the city of Lewiston in search of her mother.
   b. She wanted to scour the farm in Bybanks in search of memories.
   c. She wanted to scour the inside of the bus that skidded off the road and down the hill.
   d. She wanted to scour the school to get her journal back.

6. Where did the sheriff take Sal?
   a. He took Sal back to her grandparents.
   b. He took her to the police station where she waits for her grandparents.
   c. He took her to the scene of the bus accident.
   d. He took Sal to her mother's grave.

alk Two Moons Multiple Choice Study/Quiz Questions Chapters 40-44 (continued)

7. Who survived the bus crash?
   a. Mrs. Cadaver
   b. Sal's father
   c. Mrs. Partridge
   d. The sheriff

8. When Sal said, "This ain't your marriage bed," how did Gramps reply?"
   a. "But is sure feels like it."
   b. "It is as hard as a rock."
   c. "But it will have to do."
   d. "Ours is back home waiting for us."

9. What did Gramps name his new beagle puppy?
   a. Chickabiddy
   b. Gooseberry
   c. Blackberry
   d. Huzza Huzza

10. What was the third thing Sal was jealous of?
    a. She was jealous that her friends have siblings.
    b. She was jealous that Phoebe's mother came back while her own mother did not.
    c. She was jealous of the songbird that looks after her mother.
    d. She was jealous that Tom Fleet never wrote back to her.

ANSWER KEY - MULTIPLE CHOICE STUDY/QUIZ QUESTIONS
Walk Two Moons

	Chapters 1-5	Chapters 6-10	Chapters 11-14	Chapters 15-19	Chapters 20-23	Chapters 24-28	Chapters 29-32	Chapters 33-39	Chapters 40-44
1	C	D	B	D	D	A	A	D	A
2	B	A	A	C	A	D	D	B	D
3	B	D	D	A	B	A	A	C	C
4	D	B	D	C	B	B	B	C	C
5	C	C	A	D	A	B	D	B	C
6	A	B	B	C	D	C	D	B	D
7	A	A	C	B	D	D	B	A	A
8	D	D	A	B	A	A	C	D	C
9	B	A	C		C	C		D	D
10		D							B

PREEADING VOCABULARY WORKSHEETS

VOCABULARY CHAPTERS 1-5 *Walk Two Moons*

Part I: Using Prior Knowledge and Contextual Clues
Below are the sentences in which the vocabulary words appear in the text. Read the sentence. Use any clues you can find in the sentence combined with your prior knowledge, and write what you think the underlined words mean on the lines provided.

1. I have lived most of my thirteen years in Bybanks, Kentucky, which is not much more than a caboodle of houses roosting in a green spot alongside the Ohio River.

   _____

2. On the night that we got the bad news–that she was not returning–he pounded and pounded on that wall with a chisel and a hammer.

   _____

3. Sometimes I am as ornery and stubborn as an old donkey.

   _____

4. "I could tell you an extensively strange story, " I warned.

   _____

5. One girl, Mary Lou Finney, said the most peculiar things, like out of the blue she would say, "Omnipotent!" or "Beef brain!"

   _____

6. My mother said that Grandmother Pickford's one act of defiance in her whole life as a Pickford was in naming her.

   _____

7. A thick, gnarled cane with a handle carved in the shape of a cobra's head lay across her knees.

   _____

8. You know what cadaver means?

   _____

Walk Two Moons Vocabulary Worksheet Chapters 1-5 Continued

9. Is she the one who said I would be your <u>ruination</u>?

_____

Part II: Determining the Meaning
Match the vocabulary words to their dictionary definitions

___ 1. caboodle   A. obstinate
___ 2. chisel   B. having great extent
___ 3. ornery   C. having unlimited power
___ 4. extensively   D. a ruining or being ruined
___ 5. omnipotent   E. bold resistance to authority
___ 6. defiance   F. a hand tool with a sharp, wedged-shaped blade
___ 7. gnarled   G. a dead body
___ 8. cadaver   H. lot; group
___ 9. ruination   I. knotty and twisted, as in the trunk of an old tree

VOCABULARY CHAPTERS 6-10 *Walk Two Moons*

Part I: Using Prior Knowledge and Contextual Clues
Below are the sentences in which the vocabulary words appear in the text. Read the sentence. Use any clues you can find in the sentence combined with your prior knowledge, and write what you think the underlined words mean on the lines provided.

1. "What was the diabolic thing that happened to Mr. Cadaver?" Gramps asked.
   _____

2. They were very much concerned with cholesterol.
   _____

3. I couldn't find exactly that brand of muesli you like so much, George, but I bought something similar.
   _____

4. I felt betrayed, but I didn't know why.
   _____

5. Gramps said, "Did Gloria really have a hankering for me?"
   _____

6. He was still standing there with his hands in his pockets staring mournfully at Phoebe's house.
   _____

7. Phoebe was certain that the young man was going to ambush us.
   _____

8. It was complete pandemonium at the Finneys'.
   _____

9. Don't judge a man until you've walked two moons in his moccasins.
   _____

Walk Two Moons Vocabulary Worksheet Chapters 6-10 Continued

Part II: Determining the Meaning
Match the vocabulary words to their dictionary definitions

___ 1. diabolic
___ 2. cholesterol
___ 3. muesli
___ 4. betrayed
___ 5. hankering
___ 6. mournfully
___ 7. ambush
___ 8. pandemonium
___ 9. moccasins

A. a heelless slipper of soft, flexible leather, originally worn by North American Indians
B. suggesting sadness
C. very wicked or cruel
D. hide to make a surprise attack
E. a craving; yearning
F. deceived
G. white sterol found in animal fats that can cause blocked arteries.
H. a breakfast cereal like granola
I. wild disorder, noise, or confusion

VOCABULARY CHAPTERS 11-14 *Walk Two Moons*

Part I: Using Prior Knowledge and Contextual Clues
Below are the sentences in which the vocabulary words appear in the text. Read the sentence. Use any clues you can find in the sentence combined with your prior knowledge, and write what you think the underlined words mean on the lines provided.

1. Mary Lou thought the messages (this one and the other one) were intriguing.

   _____

2. "You don't have to get defensive," Ben said.

   _____

3. I thought it was going to be only me and Phoebe and Mary Lou going, but by the time we left the house, we had accumulated Tommy and Dougie as well.

   _____

4. When I mentioned about Ben asking where my mother was and my saying that she was in Lewiston, but that I didn't want to elaborate, Gram and Gramps looked at each other.

   _____

5. He flung himself up and down the aisles, receiving the journals as if they were manna from heaven.

   _____

6. Christy and Megan, two girls who had their own club called the GGP (whatever that meant), were whispering over on the other side of the room and casting malevolent looks in Mary Lou's direction.

   _____

7. "Deprived child," he said. "You didn't have a chance to write a journal."

   _____

8. Phoebe imagined that every noise was the lunatic sneaking in or the message-leaver creeping up to drop off another anonymous note.

Walk Two Moons Vocabulary Worksheet Chapters 11-14 Continued

9. I must have looked <u>skeptical.</u>

_____

Part II: Determining the Meaning
Match the vocabulary words to their dictionary definitions

    ____ 1. intriguing   A. not easily convinced or persuaded
    ____ 2. defensive   B. given or written by a person whose name is unknown
    ____ 3. accumulated   C. collected or gathered together
    ____ 4. elaborate   D. wishing evil or harm to others
    ____ 5. manna   E. exciting interest or curiosity
    ____ 6. malevolent   F. undergone a loss
    ____ 7. deprived   G. to add more details
    ____ 8. anonymous   H. feeling under attack and hence quick to justify one's actions
    ____ 9. skeptical   I. divine aids; spiritual sustenance

VOCABULARY CHAPTERS 15-19 *Walk Two Moons*

Part I: Using Prior Knowledge and Contextual Clues
Below are the sentences in which the vocabulary words appear in the text. Read the sentence. Use any clues you can find in the sentence combined with your prior knowledge, and write what you think the underlined words mean on the lines provided.

1. One edge <u>embedded</u> itself in the knothole.

   _____

2. The boy stopped <u>rummaging</u> through Gramps's pockets and eyed me.

   _____

3. "I guess this <u>cantankerous</u> woman is getting out of here," Gramps said.

   _____

4. She was as crotchety and <u>sullen</u> as a three-legged mule, and I was not quite sure why.

   _____

5. Besides, I was too busy throwing the most <u>colossal</u> temper tantrums.

   _____

6. The next day at school, I studied Mr. Birkway as he leaped and <u>cavorted</u> about the classroom.

   _____

7. Ben is doing an oral report on <u>Prometheus</u> this Friday.

   _____

8. You're doing one on <u>Pandora</u> next Monday.

   _____

Walk Two Moons Vocabulary Worksheet Chapters 15-19   Continued

Part II: Determining the Meaning
Match the vocabulary words to their dictionary definitions

___ 1. embedded
___ 2. rummaging
___ 3. cantankerous
___ 4. sullen
___ 5. colossal
___ 6. cavorted
___ 7. Prometheus
___ 8. Pandora

A. a Titan who steals fire from heaven for the benefit of mankind (Greek mythology)
B. pranced
C. gloomy; dismal
D. the first mortal woman; out of curiosity she opens a box (Greek mythology)
E. set or fixed firmly
F. huge; gigantic
G. quarrelsome
H. searching thoroughly by moving the contents about

VOCABULARY CHAPTERS 20-23 *Walk Two Moons*

Part I: Using Prior Knowledge and Contextual Clues
Below are the sentences in which the vocabulary words appear in the text. Read the sentence. Use any clues you can find in the sentence combined with your prior knowledge, and write what you think the underlined words mean on the lines provided.

1. Now I can see that he was just talking in general, just trying to be comforting, but then--that night--what I heard in what he said was the tiniest reassurance of something I had been thinking and hoping.

   _____

2. We have to go on with things. We can't malinger.

   _____

3. Whenever anyone tried to console me about my mother, I had nearly chomped their heads off.

   _____

4. Maybe she got knocked on the head and had amnesia and was wandering around Lewiston, not knowing who she really was, or thinking she was someone else.

   _____

5. He was worried about Gram, but less about her leg than her raspy breathing.

   _____

6. Right smack in the middle of flat plains were jagged peaks and steep gorges.

   _____

7. You can stand right on the edge of the gorges and see down, down into the most treacherous ravines, lined with sharp, rough outcroppings.

   _____

8. My mother was not a fragile, sickly woman.

   _____

9. Did she sit here in this spot and did she see that pink spire?

   _____

Walk Two Moons Vocabulary Worksheet Chapters 20-23 Continued

Part II: Determining the Meaning
Match the vocabulary words to their dictionary definitions

____ 1. reassurance
____ 2. malinger
____ 3. console
____ 4. amnesia
____ 5. raspy
____ 6. gorges
____ 7. treacherous
____ 8. fragile
____ 9. spire

A. physically weak; delicate
B. restored confidence
C. the top part of a pointed, tapering object or structure, as a mountain peak
D. to pretend to be ill to escape work
E. partial or total loss of memory caused by brain injury or shock
F. dangerously unstable
G. deep narrow passes between steep heights
H. grating; easily irritated
I. to comfort

VOCABULARY CHAPTERS 24-28 *Walk Two Moons*

Part I: Using Prior Knowledge and Contextual Clues
Below are the sentences in which the vocabulary words appear in the text. Read the sentence. Use any clues you can find in the sentence combined with your prior knowledge, and write what you think the underlined words mean on the lines provided.

1. I lay down next to her, and Gramps tentatively sat down on the other side.

2. Phoebe whispered, "I am not too optimistic about the possibilities of this meal."

3. She made her way into the kitchen, trailing all three of them like a fishhook that has snagged a tangle of old tires and boots and other miscellaneous rubbish.

4. I don't suppose you have any unadulterated vegetables?

5. Ten minutes later, Phoebe mentioned that she was getting a headache. It might even be a migraine.

6. They reminded me of my parents, before the stillborn baby, before the operation.

7. She did not have a chance to respond, because we were at her house, and she was more interested in besieging her father with questions.

8. Inside the box were all the evils in the world, such as hatred, envy, plagues, sickness, and cholesterol.

9. Oh, I would love to see Old Faithful.

Walk Two Moons Vocabulary Worksheet Chapters 24-28 Continued

Part II: Determining the Meaning
Match the vocabulary words to their dictionary definitions

___ 1. tentatively
___ 2. optimistic
___ 3. miscellaneous
___ 4. unadulterated
___ 5. migraine
___ 6. stillborn
___ 7. besieging
___ 8. plagues
___ 9. Old Faithful

A. hesitantly
B. an intense periodically returning headache
C. varied; mixed
D. harassing
E. a noted geyser in Yellowstone National Park, which erupts about every 67 minutes
F. epidemic diseases that are deadly
G. dead when delivered from the womb
H. pure
I. the tendency to expect the best outcome

VOCABULARY CHAPTERS 29-32 *Walk Two Moons*

Part I: Using Prior Knowledge and Contextual Clues
Below are the sentences in which the vocabulary words appear in the text. Read the sentence. Use any clues you can find in the sentence combined with your prior knowledge, and write what you think the underlined words mean on the lines provided.

1. She explained about her mother disappearing, and the note from Mrs. Cadaver, and Mrs. Cadaver's missing husband, and the rhododendron, and finally about the lunatic and the mysterious messages.

   _____

2. Phoebe said, "Come on," and she started up the walk. I admit I was reluctant.

   _____

3. Two chairs were covered in similar ghastly designs.

   _____

4. You don't know what you're talking about. You're being horrid.

   _____

5. It was a necessary, crucial thing to do.

   _____

6. Christy wore a pious look, as if God Himself had just come down from heaven to sit on her desk.

   _____

7. I think he hypnotized her, because Beth Ann sat down slowly.

   _____

8. When the bell rang, people went berserk.

   _____

Walk Two Moons Vocabulary Worksheet Chapters 29-32 Continued

Part II: Determining the Meaning
Match the vocabulary words to their dictionary definitions

____ 1. rhododendron
____ 2. reluctant
____ 3. ghastly
____ 4. horrid
____ 5. crucial
____ 6. pious
____ 7. hypnotized
____ 8. berserk

A. having or showing religious devotion
B. in a state of violent or destructive rage or frenzy
C. put into a trance-like condition
D. horrible; frightful
E. a shrub with showy flowers of pink, white, or purple
F. of supreme importance
G. causing a feeling of horror; ugly; unpleasant
H. unwilling

VOCABULARY CHAPTERS 33-39 *Walk Two Moons*

Part I: Using Prior Knowledge and Contextual Clues
Below are the sentences in which the vocabulary words appear in the text. Read the sentence. Use any clues you can find in the sentence combined with your prior knowledge, and write what you think the underlined words mean on the lines provided.

1. I watched it plunge on, eating up the road, <u>defying</u> those curves.

_____

2. In English class, everyone <u>badgered</u> Mr. Birkway to finish reading the journal entry that he had begun yesterday, the one about Mrs. Corpse and the body, but Mr. Birkway did not read any more journals.

_____

3. Every time I was with him now, my skin tickled and my brain buzzed and my blood romped around as if it were <u>percolating</u>.

_____

4. What I did next was an <u>impulse</u>.

_____

5. "She said to tell you not to make any <u>prejudgments</u>."

_____

6. They've scrubbed floors and bathrooms, they dusted like <u>fiends</u>, they did laundry and ironing, and they vacuumed.

_____

7. Mrs. Winterbottom looked too terrific to have been held <u>captive</u>.

_____

8. Then he did what I think was a <u>noble</u> thing.

_____

Walk Two Moons Vocabulary Worksheet Chapters 33-39 Continued

Part II: Determining the Meaning
Match the vocabulary words to their dictionary definitions

___ 1. defying
___ 2. badgered
___ 3. percolating
___ 4. impulse
___ 5. prejudgments
___ 6. fiends
___ 7. captive
___ 8. noble

A. an impelling force
B. challenging; daring
C. judgments without all the evidence
D. pestered
E. persons addicted to some activity; habit
F. taken or held prisoner
G. showing high moral qualities
H. bubbling up

VOCABULARY CHAPTERS 40-44 *Walk Two Moons*

Part I: Using Prior Knowledge and Contextual Clues
Below are the sentences in which the vocabulary words appear in the text. Read the sentence. Use any clues you can find in the sentence combined with your prior knowledge, and write what you think the underlined words mean on the lines provided.

1. "Your momma sent us a postcard from Coeur d'Alene, and on it was a bountiful blue lake."

   _____

2. Gramps insisted on being with her while she underwent tests, though an intern had tried to dissuade him.

   _____

3. She's weaning them from her.

   _____

4. Between me and Lewiston was the treacherous road with its hairpin turns that twisted back and forth down the mountain.

   _____

5. "I don't suppose you would mind telling me exactly what was so all-fired important that you couldn't wait for someone with a legitimate driver's license to bring you to the fair city of Lewiston?"

   _____

6. He settled his hat on his head and shifted his holster.

   _____

7. Nine hours after that bus rolled over, as all those stretchers were being carried up the hill, and everyone despairing – there was her hand coming up out of the window and everyone was shouting because there it was, a moving hand.

   _____

8. He was too grief-stricken, and he was trying to spare me.

   _____

Walk Two Moons Vocabulary Worksheet Chapters 40-44 Continued

Part II: Determining the Meaning
Match the vocabulary words to their dictionary definitions

___ 1. bountiful
___ 2. dissuade
___ 3. weaning
___ 4. hairpin
___ 5. legitimate
___ 6. holster
___ 7. despairing
___ 8. spare

A. U-shaped
B. giving up hope
C. legal
D. refrain from troubling or worrying
E. plentiful
F. adapting a young child or a young animal to go without something
G. a holder for a pistol
H. persuade against (an action)

VOCABULARY ANSWER KEY
Walk Two Moons

	Chapters 1-5	Chapters 6-10	Chapters 11-14	Chapters 15-19	Chapters 20-23	Chapters 24-28	Chapters 29-32	Chapters 33-39	Chapters 40-44
1	H	C	E	E	B	A	E	B	E
2	F	G	H	H	D	I	H	D	H
3	A	H	C	G	I	C	D	H	F
4	B	F	G	C	E	H	G	A	A
5	C	E	I	F	H	B	F	C	C
6	E	B	D	B	G	G	A	E	G
7	I	D	F	A	F	D	C	F	B
8	G	I	B	D	A	F	B	G	D
9	D	A	A		C	E			

DAILY LESSONS

LESSON ONE

Objectives
1. To introduce students to the book *Walk Two Moons*
2. To discuss the concept of change and how it affects people differently
3. To connect the introductory activity with the book
4. To distribute the materials students will need in this unit

Activity #1
Brainstorm with students possible life changes a person may encounter. Encourage them to share their experiences with change and to describe how the experiences made them feel. Mention how change can also be viewed as a loss or an opportunity. Elaborate on how everyone encounters change and/or loss in their lives and how it affects people differently. Help them to realize that the amount of control you have over the change can also affect how you respond to it.

Activity #2
Place students into groups of three. Give each group an index card with a life change written on it. Have students write down how the change may affect a person and his/her family and friends. Also have them write down coping strategies the person could use. Allow time for groups to share their responses. Suggested changes could include: a serious injury or illness; a move to a new home, school, or community; learning a new skill; a new family member; a big vacation; problems with friends or family; death of a family member or a friend.

Activity #3
After each group has shared their responses, tell students that the book they will be reading is about a girl, Salamanca Tree Hiddle, who must face and come to terms with major changes in her life, some of which *they* may have experienced. Describe how Salamanca's (Sal) life story unfolds as she tells a story to her grandparents. Point out that the book is a winner of the Newbery Medal.

Activity #4
Distribute the books and materials students will use in this unit. Allow time for students to preview the book. Tell them you will explain how to use the materials in the next lesson.

Study Guides Students should read the study guide questions for each reading assignment prior to beginning the reading assignment to get a feeling for what events and ideas are important in the section they are about to read. After reading the section, students will (as a class or individually) answer the questions to review the important events and ideas from that section of the book. Students should keep the study guides as study materials for the unit test.

Vocabulary Prior to each reading assignment, students will do vocabulary work related to the section of the book they are about to read. Following the completion of the reading of the book, there will be a vocabulary review of all the words used in the vocabulary assignments. Students should keep their vocabulary work as study materials for the unit test.

Reading Assignment Sheet   You need to fill in the reading assignment sheet to let students know by when their reading has to be completed. You can either write the assignment sheet up on a side blackboard or bulletin board and leave it there for students to see each day, or you can "ditto" copies for each student to have. In either case, you should advise students to become very familiar with the reading assignments so they know what is expected of them.

Extra Activities Center   The Unit Resource Materials portion of this LitPlan contains suggestions for an extra library of related books and articles in your classroom as well as crossword and word search puzzles. Make an extra activities center in your room where you will keep these materials for students to use. (Bring the books and articles in from the library and keep several copies of the puzzles on hand.) Explain to students that these materials are available for students to use when they finish reading assignments or other class work early.

Nonfiction Assignment Sheet   Explain to students that they each are to read at least one nonfiction piece from the in-class library at some time during the unit. Students will fill out a nonfiction assignment sheet after completing the reading to help you (the teacher) evaluate their reading experiences and to help the students think about and evaluate their own reading experiences.

Books   Each school has its own rules and regulations regarding student use of school books. Advise students of the procedures that are normal for your school.

LESSON TWO

Objectives
1. To show students how to use the materials relating to the unit
2. To acquaint students with the vocabulary for chapters 1-5
3. To preview chapters 1-5
4. To read chapters 1-5
5. To evaluate students' oral reading

Activity #1

Tell students to look at the materials you distributed, and discuss how the materials are to be used.

Activity #2

Read through the study questions with your students. Explain to them that they should read the questions prior to doing the reading of each assignment so they have some clues about what will be important in their reading.

Activity #3

Do the vocabulary worksheet for chapters 1-5 orally, together, as a class to show students how the worksheets are to be completed. Explain that students will do one of these for each reading assignment in this unit.

Activity #4

Begin the reading of the book. Have your students read orally so you can evaluate their oral reading. You probably know the best way to get readers with your class; pick students at random, ask for volunteers, or use whatever method works best for your group.

For your convenience, an oral reading evaluation form follows. Duplicate the form and use one for each student.

If students do not finish reading chapters 1-5 in class, they should do so for homework.

ORAL READING EVALUATION *Walk Two Moons*

Name _____ Class____ Date_____

SKILL	EXCELLENT	GOOD	AVERAGE	FAIR	POOR
Fluency	5	4	3	2	1
Clarity	5	4	3	2	1
Audibility	5	4	3	2	1
Pronunciation	5	4	3	2	1
_____	5	4	3	2	1
_____	5	4	3	2	1

Total _____   Grade _____

Comments:

LESSON THREE

Objectives
1. To review the main ideas and events from chapters 1-5
2. To preview and read chapters 6-10

Activity #1
Give students a few minutes to formulate answers for the study guide questions for chapters 1-5, and then discuss the answers to the questions in detail. Write the answers on the board or overhead transparency so students can have the correct answers for study purposes.

Notes:
Answering the study questions for each section can get boring if it is done the same way every time. You might consider varying the ways it is done throughout the unit. For example students could write the answers as independent work, formulate answers in small groups or pairs, formulate answers as a class, or answer the questions as a quiz. If answers are formulated in any way other than the whole class doing so orally, be sure to gather the class together to discuss the answers so all students do have the correct answers for study purposes.

It is a good practice in public speaking and leadership skills for individual students to take charge of leading the discussions of the study questions. Perhaps a different student or pairs/groups of students could go to the front of the class and lead the discussion each day that the study questions are discussed during this unit. Of course, the teacher should guide the discussion when appropriate and be sure to fill in any gaps the students leave.

Activity #2
Give students time to preview the study questions and do the vocabulary worksheet for chapters 6-10. Whether you discuss the vocabulary answers or simply make the answer key available on the board for students to check their own work after they have had ample time to complete it, just be sure that they do get the right answers for study purposes.

Activity #3
If you did not complete the oral reading evaluations in the last class meeting, continue them as students read chapters 6-10. If you did complete them, students may read silently or in pairs (taking turns reading to each other). This reading assignment should be completed prior to the next class meeting.

LESSON FOUR

Objectives
1. To review the main ideas and events of chapters 6-10
2. To preview the study questions and vocabulary for chapters 11-14
3. To discuss the effects of prejudgments on others
4. To have students practice writing to persuade
5. To evaluate students' writing skills
6. To get students to consider the relevance of passages in the book to their own lives

Activity #1
Have students formulate answers to the study questions for chapters 6-10 and discuss the answers, as directed in Lesson Three.

Activity #2
Segue into a discussion to introduce the first writing assignment by asking students, "Have you ever prejudged someone?" Discuss how a prejudgment is an opinion, a feeling, or an attitude that is often incorrect because one does not know the person or have all the facts about a situation. Have students think of ways that *people* can be prejudged. Ask questions to help them include the many ways one can prejudge others such as by: gender, looks, attire, intelligence, not being in the "in crowd," ethnicity, age, and economic status. Also ask students if it is ever helpful to prejudge another.

Have them reflect upon the ways prejudgments about people have appeared in *Walk Two Moons*. Provide 5 or 10 minutes for students to find examples in the text such as Sal and Phoebe's attitudes toward Mrs. Cadaver and Phoebe's feeling about the young man at the door.
Provide time for students to share examples with the class.

Lead into a discussion about the quote, "Don't judge a man until you've walked two moon in his moccasins." (end of chapter 10) Allow time for students to reflect upon this quote and how it ties in with prejudgments.

Activity #3
Distribute Writing Assignment #1, discuss the directions in detail, and give students ample time to complete the assignment. Tell students whether the assignment is due at the end of this class meeting or at another time. Collect it accordingly.

There is time in Lesson Fourteen for you to have writing conferences with students. Filling out a Writing Evaluation Form as you grade this writing assignment will give you a good basis for the writing conference.

Activity #4
If students finish the writing assignment early, they should do the prereading work (preview the study questions and do the vocabulary worksheet) for chapters 11-14. The prereading work should be done as homework if students do not finish it in class.

WRITING ASSIGNMENT #1 *Walk Two Moons*
Writing to Persuade

PROMPT
You have found examples of characters prejudging others in *Walk Two Moons*. There are many ways a person can prejudge others including by gender, looks, attire, intelligence, not being in the "in crowd," ethnicity, age, and economic status. Consider a time when someone prejudged you. When did the experience occur? How did it make you feel? Your assignment is to write a persuasive letter to convince the person who prejudged you that he/she was wrong. In order for you to write more freely, use a fictional name for the person you are writing to.

PREWRITING
Try to remember your reactions to the prejudgment. How did it make you feel? What emotions did you experience? Why did the person prejudge you? In what ways was he/she wrong? How are you going to convince the person he/she was wrong? Jot down your notes about these things.

DRAFTING
Describe the experience in the first paragraph. The body paragraphs of the letter should include reasons why the person was wrong about you. Think about including personal interests, experiences, and beliefs that may help the person get to know you better. The final paragraph (closing) should restate your strongest persuasive points to leave a lasting impression about why the person prejudged you incorrectly.

PROOFREADING
Upon completion, read your writing out loud. Reading aloud will help you hear what your eye did not see. After reading aloud, double-check your grammar, spelling, organization, and the clarity of your ideas. If possible, put your paper aside for a short duration, then proofread it one more time before handing it in.

WRITING EVALUATION FORM - *Walk Two Moons*

Name _____ Date _____

Grade _____

Circle One For Each Item:

Grammar: correct errors noted on paper

Spelling: correct errors noted on paper

Punctuation: correct errors noted on paper

Legibility: excellent   good   fair   poor

_____ excellent   good   fair   poor

_____ excellent   good   fair   poor

Strengths:

Weaknesses:

Comments/Suggestions:

LESSON FIVE

Objectives
    1. To check the vocabulary work from chapters 11-14
    2. To read chapters 11-14
    3. To give students the opportunity to finish Writing Assignment #1 (if they did not do so in the last class period)

Activity #1
    Tell students to look at their vocabulary worksheets for chapters 11-14. Have students exchange papers to correct. Briefly discuss the correct answers so students have the right ones to study from.

Activity #2
    Students should use this class period to read chapters 11-14. If you have not completed the oral reading evaluations, do so today. If you have finished, students may read silently or in groups. This assignment should be completed as homework if not finished in class.

    If you did not collect the writing assignments in the last class period, students should finish those prior to reading chapters 11-14.

LESSON SIX

Objectives
1. To review the main ideas and events from chapters 11-14
2. To preview the study questions for chapters 15-19
3. To complete the vocabulary work from chapters 15-19
3. To read chapters 15-19

Activity #1
Discuss the study questions for chapters 11-14 as directed in Lesson Three.

Activity #2
Have students look at their study questions and vocabulary worksheets for chapters 15-19. Preview the questions, and do the vocabulary together as a class.

Activity #3
Students should use the remainder of the period to read chapters 15-19. This reading assignment should be completed prior to the next meeting.

LESSON SEVEN

Objectives
1. To review the main ideas and event of chapters 15-19
2. To check students' knowledge of chapters 1-19
3. To discuss Sharon Creech's writing style
4. To find examples of similes and idioms

Activity #1

Discuss the study questions for chapters 15-19 as directed in Lesson Three.

Activity #2

Distribute the quizzes for chapters 1-19. Give students ample time to complete them, then have students swap papers for grading. Discuss the answers as students grade the papers. Collect the quizzes for recording the grades.

Activity #3

After the quizzes have been collected, initiate a discussion about the author's writing style, specifically the use of similes and idioms.

Review the definitions of the two terms: A simile is a comparison using like or as. Idioms are phrases or expressions that cannot be taken literally. They have meanings other than the ones you would find in the dictionary.

In pairs, have students find examples of similes and idioms from chapters 1-19. A few examples from chapter 2 include: "Sometimes I am as ornery and stubborn as an old donkey." "Once it was settled that the three of us would go, the journey took on an alarming, expanding need to hurry that was like a walloping great thundercloud assembling around me." "My father says I lean on broken reeds and will get a face full of swamp mud one day." "There was certainly a hog's belly full of things to tell about her."

Have students share examples with the class. Record them for use on a bulletin board or a writing information center. Further explore the use and meanings of selected idioms and similes and how they provide voice and insight about the characters. Encourage students to write down other examples as they continue to read the story.

MULTIPLE CHOICE QUIZ CHAPTERS 1-19 *Walk Two Moons*

1. Who was Sal locked in a car with for six days?
    a. Phoebe Winterbottom
    b. Her grandparents
    c. Her father
    d. Margaret Cadaver

2. Once Sal decided to go on the trip, she prayed she would be in Idaho by when?
    a. She prayed she would be in Idaho before it started to snow.
    b. She prayed she would be in Idaho before the start of the school year.
    c. She prayed she would be in Idaho by her mother's birthday.
    d. She prayed she would be in Idaho before she turned fourteen.

3. What did Phoebe think about Mrs. Cadaver?
    a. Phoebe thought Mrs. Cadaver killed Mr. Cadaver, chopped him up, and buried him in the backyard.
    b. Phoebe thought Mrs. Cadaver stole jewelry from Mrs. Finney.
    c. Phoebe thought Mrs. Cadaver was a noisy neighbor who spied on people in the neighborhood.
    d. Phoebe thought Mrs. Cadaver was a famous artist who moved to the neighborhood for privacy.

4. Who drew a picture of Sal as a lizard-like creature with long black hair?
    a. Ben Finney
    b. Phoebe
    c. Mary Lou Finney
    d. The boy that sits next to her in school

5. What secret did Mrs. Winterbottom want to keep from Mr. Winterbottom?
    a. She does not want to tell him she lost her job at Rocky's Rubber.
    b. She does not want to tell him about the fight between Phoebe and Prudence.
    c. She does not want to tell him about the money she found at the park.
    d. She does not want to tell him about the boy who stopped by the house.

6. Why did Gramps purchase Sal a peace pipe?
    a. He wanted Sal to give it to her father.
    b. Gramps believed it would keep Sal safe.
    c. He wanted Sal to keep it for him.
    d. He told her, "It's for remembering with."

Walk Two Moons Quiz Chapters 1-19 Continued

7. Who was Mr. Birkway?
   a. Sal's physician
   b. Sal's teacher
   c. Gramps' best friend
   d. Phoebe's uncle

8. "We had absolutely no idea all the trouble they were going to cause." To what did this statement refer?
   a. The peace pipes Gramps purchased
   b. The cartoons Ben drew
   c. The journals Mr. Birkway collected
   d. The articles in the newspaper about Mrs. Cadaver

9. Sal's mother said she had to leave in order to do what?
   a. She wanted to get away from Bybanks and "see the world."
   b. She wanted to "find happiness by being an inspiration to others."
   c. She wanted to clear her head and "to clear her heart of all the bad things."
   d. She wanted to "restore the shattered relationship with her parents and siblings."

10. Sal's mother left Sal a good-bye letter. In the letter, when did she say she would return?
    a. Before the snow falls
    b. Before the tulips bloom
    c. Before Sal's birthday
    d. Before summer vacation

MULTIPLE CHOICE QUIZ ANSWERS   CHAPTERS 1-19   *Walk Two Moons*

1. B
2. C
3. A
4. A
5. D
6. D
7. B
8. C
9. C
10. B

SHORT ANSWER QUIZ CHAPTERS 1-19 *Walk Two Moons*

1. Who was Sal locked in a car with for six days?

2. Once Sal decided to go on the trip, she prayed she would be in Idaho by when?

3. What did Phoebe think about Mrs. Cadaver?

4. Who drew a picture of Sal as a lizard-like creature with long black hair?

5. What secret did Mrs. Winterbottom want to keep from Mr. Winterbottom?

6. Why did Gramps purchase Sal a peace pipe?

7. Who was Mr. Birkway?

8. "We had absolutely no idea all the trouble they were going to cause." To what did this statement refer?

9. Sal's mother said she had to leave in order to do what?

10. Sal's mother left Sal a good-bye letter. In the letter, when did she say she would return?

SHORT ANSWER QUIZ ANSWERS 1-19 *Walk Two Moons*

1. Who was Sal locked in a car with for six days?
    She was locked in a car with her grandparents.

2. Once Sal decided to go on the trip, she prayed she would be in Idaho by when?
    She prayed to get to Idaho by her mother's birthday.

3. What did Phoebe think about Mrs. Cadaver?
    Phoebe thought Mrs. Cadaver killed Mr. Cadaver, chopped him up, and buried him in the backyard.

4. Who drew a picture of Sal as a lizard-like creature with long black hair?
    Ben Finney drew it.

5. What secret did Mrs. Winterbottom want to keep from Mr. Winterbottom?
    She did not want to tell him about the boy who stopped by the house.

6. Why did Gramps purchase Sal a peace pipe?
    He told Sal, "It's for remembering with."

7. Who was Mr. Birkway?
    Mr. Birkway was Sal's teacher.

8. "We had absolutely no idea all the trouble they were going to cause." To what did this statement refer?
    This statement referred to the journals Mr. Birkway collected.

9. Sal's mother said she had to leave in order to do what?
    She wanted to clear her head and "to clear her heart of all the bad things." She also wanted to learn about what she was on her own.

10. Sal's mother left Sal a good-bye letter. In the letter, when did she say she would return?
    She said she would return before the tulips bloom.

LESSON EIGHT

Objectives
1. To introduce the group unit project
2. To review the requirements of the group project
3. To preview the study questions and vocabulary for chapters 20-23
4. To check the vocabulary work from chapters 20-23
5. To read chapters 20-23

Activity #1

Tell students they will be working on a group project that focuses on the sites Sal and her grandparents visited on their way to Idaho. At this time, either assign or randomly select group members. Depending on class size, you may have more than one group researching the same site.

Activity #2

Distribute the non-fiction assignment sheet that details the cooperative group project requirements. Explain how they will research one of the national parks or monuments from Sal's trip. They will research the park's history, activities, climate, and most importantly its association with Native Americans. Group members will also assume Sal's identity by writing a fictional account of "Sal's" impressions and experiences at the park (other than those already reported in *Walk Two Moons*).

Assign one of the following to each group:
Badlands National Park
Mt. Rushmore National Memorial
Pipestone National Monument
Yellowstone National Park

Describe to students how they will conduct research in the media center by consulting at least two different non-fiction sources. Reliable sources include books, magazines, the internet (the National Park Service has websites for each park, memorial, or monument), videos, or any other reliable sources. Let them know that upon completion each group will share their information and journal entry with the class.

Activity #3

Allow students to remain in groups to do the pre-reading work for chapters 20-23. After they have completed the work, briefly discuss the answers to the vocabulary worksheet.

Activity #4

Students should use the remainder of the class period to read chapters 20-23. The reading should be completed prior to the next class meeting.

SAL'S JOURNEY WEST

Name of Park or Monument _____

Map: You must provide a map that outlines Sal's journey from Euclid, Ohio to your assigned Park. The map must also include all the stops she and her grandparents made prior to reaching your Park.

History of Park, Monument, or Memorial:

Climate:

Activities and Events:

Fascinating Facts:

Association with Native Americans:

Journal Entry: Assume Sal's identity by writing a fictional account of "Sal's" impressions and experiences at your site (other than those already reported in *Walk Two Moons*).

Source 1:

Source 2:

LESSON NINE

Objectives
1. To review the main ideas and events of chapters 20-23
2. To preview the study questions and vocabulary for chapters 24-28
3. To read chapters 24-28

Activity #1
Discuss the answers to the study questions for chapters 20-23 as directed in Lesson Three.

Activity #2
Preview the study questions for chapters 24-28, do the vocabulary work, and read chapters 24-28. This assignment should be completed prior to the next class meeting.

LESSON TEN

Objectives
1. To review the main ideas and events of chapters 24-28
2. To check the vocabulary from chapters 24-28
3. To work on the group project

Activity #1
Discuss the answers to the study questions for chapters 24-28 as directed in Lesson Three. Review the answers to the vocabulary worksheet.

Activity #2
Devote the remainder of the class period to the group research project outlined in Lesson Eight.

LESSON ELEVEN

Objectives
1. To preview the study questions and vocabulary for chapters 29-32
2. To read chapters 29-32
3. To work on the group project
4. To share the group project evaluation

Activity #1
Preview the study questions for chapters 29-32, do the vocabulary work, and read chapters 29-32.

Activity #2
Devote the remainder of the class period to the group project. Distribute copies of the group project evaluation for students to read so they know how their peers will assess them during the oral presentation.

Group Project Evaluation
Sal's Journey West

Name of Group_____

	Very Good	Satisfactory	Needs to Improve
Presented all the information: history, climate, activities, facts, and Native American association			
Map outlined Sal's journey from Euclid, Ohio to assigned destination			
Group members maintained eye contact and spoke clearly			
All group members participated in the presentation			
Journal entry portrays a realistic fictional account of Sal's impressions and experiences			

Comments:

LESSON TWELVE

Objectives
1. To review the main ideas and events of chapters 29-32
2. To check the vocabulary from chapters 29-32
3. To analyze the poems featured in *Walk Two Moons*
4. To have students practice writing to inform

Activity #1
Discuss the answers to the study questions for chapters 29-32 as directed in Lesson Three. Review the answers to the vocabulary worksheet.

Activity #2
Recall how Mr. Birkway reads two poems—"The Tide Rises, the Tide Falls" by Henry Wadsworth Longfellow (Chapter 29) and "The Little Horse is NewlY" by e.e. cummings (chapter 20) that affect Sal. **Obtain copies of the poems**, and distribute them to the students. Read the poems aloud, and discuss students' reactions to them. What do the poems mean? Is there anything left unsaid in the poems? What are the implied meanings? How did Sal react to the poems? Why did Phoebe, Megan, Ben and Sal have different reactions to "The Tide Rises, the Tide Falls?" What happens to the traveler? Talk about how each person brings a different interpretation to the poem based on his/her life experiences. Tell them they will share their interpretations of the poem in the next writing assignment.

Activity #3
Distribute Writing Assignment #2. Explain the directions, and tell students they will have time to continue writing tomorrow too. Filling out a Writing Evaluation Form as you grade this writing assignment will give you a good basis for the writing conference in Lesson Fourteen.

Writing Assignment #2 *Walk Two Moons*
Writing to Inform

PROMPT
Mr. Birkway reads two poems in *Walk Two Moons*: "The Little Horse is NewlY" by e.e. cummings and "The Tide Rises, The Tide Falls" by Henry Wadsworth Longfellow. Sal responds to each of the poems. However, her reaction to Longfellow's poem is quite different than Megan's, Ben's and Mary Lou's reactions. As you have learned, each individual brings personal meaning to poetry based on life experiences. Now it's your turn to respond. Select one of the two poems and explain what it means to you.

PREWRITING
How did Sal respond to the poems? What in her life made her react the way she did? What do you think the poet is trying to say? Why do you think that? Is there anything left unsaid? What is the poet implying? What feelings does the poem give you? Why? Jot down your thoughts about these things.

DRAFTING
Describe your reactions in the first paragraph. The body paragraphs should include reasons why you feel the way you do. Use examples from the poem. Also include your thoughts on the setting and the rhythm. The final paragraph/closing should restate why you feel the way you do based on the literal and the implied text of the poem.

PROOFREADING
When you finish the rough draft of your explanation, ask a student who sits near you to read it. After reading your rough draft, he/she should tell you what she/he liked best about it, which parts were difficult to understand, and ways in which your work could be improved. Reread your paper considering your critic's comments, and make the corrections you think are necessary. Do a final proofreading of your paper by double-checking your grammar, spelling, organization, and the clarity of your ideas.

LESSON THIRTEEN

Objectives
1. To preview the study questions and vocabulary for chapters 33-39
2. To read chapters 33-39
3. To finish writing assignment #2

Activity #1
Preview the study questions for chapters 33-39, do the vocabulary work, and read chapters 33-39.

Activity #2
When students finish reading, they should complete Writing Assignment #2. Make another set of Writing Evaluation Forms to use when grading this assignment. Tell students the reading and writing assignments are due tomorrow.

LESSON FOURTEEN

Objectives
1. To review the vocabulary, main ideas and events from chapters 33-39
2. To evaluate students' writing skills
3. To work on the group project

Activity #1
Discuss the answers to the vocabulary worksheet, and discuss the study questions for chapters 33- 39 as directed in Lesson Three.

Activity #2
Devote the remainder of the class period to the group project. Tell students they will have one more opportunity to meet as a group. While students are working on the project, have individual writing conferences with students who have finished Writing Assignment #2.

LESSON FIFTEEN

Objectives
1. To preview the study questions and vocabulary for chapters 40-44
2. To read chapters 40-44
3. To evaluate students' writing skills
4. To work on the group project

Activity #1
Preview the study questions for chapters 40-44, do the vocabulary work, and read chapters 40-44.

Activity #2
When students finish reading, they should meet one more time to finalize their group projects. While students work on the project, continue the writing conferences for Writing Assignment #2. Group projects will be presented in Lesson Eighteen.

LESSONS SIXTEEN AND SEVENTEEN

Objectives
1. To review the vocabulary, the main ideas, and the events from chapters 40-44
2. To answer higher-level comprehension questions including interpretation, critical analysis and personal response
3. To use a variety of thinking skills that add to the understanding of the novel
4. To discuss the answers to the questions

Activity #1
Discuss the answers to the vocabulary worksheet, and discuss the study questions for chapters 40-44 as directed in Lesson Three.

Activity #2
Choose the questions from the Extra Discussion Questions/Writing Assignments which seem most appropriate for your students. A class discussion of these questions is most effective if students have been given the opportunity to formulate answers to the questions prior to the discussion. Therefore, you may either have all the students formulate answers to all the questions, divide your class into groups and assign one or more questions to each group, or you could assign one question to each student in your class. The option you choose will make a difference in the amount of class time needed for this activity. Also, review the significance of the selected quotations which appear on the unit test.

NOTE: The use of graphic organizers may be helpful to students in preparing their answers. Encourage them to use any diagrams or graphics that they feel are necessary.

EXTRA WRITING ASSIGNMENTS/DISCUSSION QUESTIONS *Walk Two Moons*

Interpretation
1. Describe Sal's relationship with Phoebe.
2. What are the main conflicts in the story? Are they all resolved by the end of the story?
3. How do the places Sal visits with her grandparents enhance the story?
4. Where is the high point (climax) of the story?
5. Describe Sharon Creech's writing style. How does it affect the story?
6. Why did Mr. Birkway read the student journals to the class?
7. Why did Mrs. Winterbottom leave home without telling anyone?
8. Name some lessons Sal learned on her trip to Idaho.
9. How would you describe Sal's personality?

Critical
1. In what ways does telling the story of Phoebe help Sal?
2. Why is the book entitled *Walk Two Moons*?
3. Compare and contrast Phoebe's family to Mary Lou's family.
4. Explain the significance of Sal's relationship to her grandparents.
5. What does Phoebe gain from Sal's friendship?
6. How does Sal change from the beginning of the book to the end of the book?
7. How does the myth of Pandora's box tie into the story?
8. Compare and contrast Gram and Gramps.
9. How does Phoebe's story help the reader understand Sal's story?
10. Compare and contrast Phoebe and Sal. Compare and contrast their mothers.
11. What was the purpose of the "doorstep messages?"
11. How did the author foreshadow Gram's death?
12. Explain the significance of the singing tree.
13. How are Sal and her mother the same? How are they different?
14. Why did Sal dislike Mrs. Cadaver?
15. How does the author's use of dialect and idioms provide voice to the characters?

Critical/Personal Response
1. Why did the author choose to tell two stories?
2. Why do you think Sal's mother left?
3. Should Gramps have allowed Sal to drive alone to Lewiston, Idaho?
4. Do you think Mrs. Winterbottom led a "tiny life" prior to meeting her son?

Walk Two Moons Extra Discussion Questions Continued

Personal Response
1. What was your reaction to the book? Did you like it? Would your recommend it?
2. Did you find the characters believable?
3. What do you think happens to Sal, her father, and Gramps after the book ends?
4. Do you think Mr. and Mrs. Winterbottom remain married? Why or why not?
5. Do you think the book should have won the Newbery Medal? Why or why not?
6. Should Sharon Creech write a sequel? Why or why not?
7. Gram frequently said, "Huzza, Huzza." What expressions do members of your family use a lot?
8. Would you want to be friends with Sal? Why or why not?

Quotations
1. "I realized that the story of Phoebe was like the plaster wall in our old house in Bybanks, Kentucky." (Chapter 1)
2. "My father says I lean on broken reeds and will get a face full of swamp mud one day." (Chapter 1)
3. "What I have since realized is that if people expect you to be brave, sometimes you pretend that you are, even when you are frightened down to your very bones." (Chapter 3)
4. "Don't judge a man until you've walked two moons in his moccasins." (Chapter 9)
5. "Being a mother is like trying to hold a wolf by the ears." (Chapter 10)
6. "Everyone has his own agenda." (Chapter 11)
7. "In the course of a lifetime, what does it matter?" (Chapter 17)
8. "Sal, you're trying to catch fish in the air." (Chapter 19)
9. "A person isn't a bird. You can't cage a person." (Chapter 22)
10. "Sometimes you know in your heart you love someone, but you have to go away before your head can figure it out." (Chapter 24)
11. "You can't keep the birds of sadness from flying over your head, but you can keep them from nesting in your hair." (Chapter 24)
12. "Once, before she left, my mother said that if you visualize something happening, you can make it happen." (Chapter 30)
13. "We never know the worth of water, until the well is dry." (Chapter 31)
14. "I decided that bravery is looking Pandora's box full in the eye as best you can, and then turning to the other box, the one with the smoothbeautiful folds: . . ." (Chapter 44)

LESSON EIGHTEEN

Objectives
1. To share the group project research and journal entry
2. To present information orally

Activity #1

Have each group share the results of their national park research and their fictional journal entry. While each group presents, their peers will evaluate their presentation using the group project evaluation. After all the presentations, hold a brief class discussion about the information students have just heard. Collect the evaluations. You may choose to complete an evaluation sheet for each group yourself.

LESSON NINETEEN

Objectives
1. To have students practice writing their personal opinions
2. To evaluate students' writing skills
3. To bring the unit to a conclusion

Activity #1

Discuss the following quotation from chapter 17. "As I walked home, I thought about the message. In the course of a lifetime, what does it matter? I said it over and over. I wondered about the mysterious messenger, and I thought about all the things in the course of a lifetime that would not matter. I did not think cheerleading tryouts would matter, but I was not so sure about yelling at your mother. I was certain, however, that if your mother left, it would be something that mattered in the whole long course of your lifetime."

How is Sal feeling when she thinks about the message? What is she implying? What types of things do not matter over the course of a lifetime? What things do matter? Are they the same for everyone? What matters to you in the course of a lifetime?

Activity #2

Distribute Writing Assignment #3. Discuss the directions in detail, and give students ample time to complete the assignment. Collect the assignment for grading.

Writing Assignment #3 *Walk Two Moons*
Writing Personal Opinions

PROMPT

In chapter 17, Sal thinks about the message, "**In the course of a lifetime, what does it matter?**" She wonders if Prudence's preoccupation with cheerleading tryouts would matter. The same message seems to have an significant impact on Mrs. Winterbottom. However, her daughters do not notice their mother's reaction due to their "own agendas."

How can you apply this message to your own life? What matters to you over the course of a lifetime? What things do not matter?

Your assignment is to write an essay in which you state and explain your standards for what *is* as well as what *is not* important in life.

PREWRITING

Make a list of what is important to you in life. Think about family, friends, future goals, how you spend your time, and whatever else may hold personal significance. Make another list of what is not important to you. Compare the two. Use the two lists as springboards to explain what matters to you and why.

DRAFTING

Explain what the quote means in the first paragraph. The body of the paper should explain what matters to you over the course of a lifetime and why. Also, include your thoughts about what does not matter. The final paragraph/closing should restate why you feel the way you do at this point in your life.

PROOFREADING

Upon completion, read your writing out loud. Reading aloud will help you hear what your eye did not see. After reading aloud, double-check your grammar, spelling, organization, and the clarity of your ideas. If possible, put your paper aside for a short duration, then proofread it one more time before handing it in.

LESSON TWENTY

Objective
    To pull together and review all of the vocabulary work done in this unit

Activity
    Choose one (or more) of the vocabulary review activities listed below and spend your class period as directed in the activity. Some of the materials for these review activities are located in the Vocabulary Resource Materials section in this LitPlan.

VOCABULARY REVIEW ACTIVITIES

1. Divide your class into two teams and have an old-fashioned spelling or definition bee.

2. Give each of your students (or students in groups of two, three or four) a *Walk Two Moons* Vocabulary Word Search Puzzle. The person (group) to find all of the vocabulary words in the puzzle first wins.

3. Give students a *Walk Two Moons* Vocabulary Word Search Puzzle without the word list. The person or group to find the most vocabulary words in the puzzle wins.

4. Use a *Walk Two Moons* Vocabulary Crossword Puzzle. Put the puzzle onto a transparency on the overhead projector (so everyone can see it), and do the puzzle together as a class.

5. Give students a *Walk Two Moons* Vocabulary Matching Worksheet to do.

6. Divide your class into two teams. Use *Walk Two Moons* vocabulary words with their letters jumbled as a word list. Student 1 from Team A faces off against Student 1 from Team B. You write the first jumbled word on the board. The first student (1A or 1B) to unscramble the word wins the chance for his/her team to score points. If 1A wins the jumble, go to student 2A and give him/her a definition. He/she must give you the correct spelling of the vocabulary word which fits that definition. If he/she does, Team A scores a point, and you give student 3A a definition for which you expect a correctly spelled matching vocabulary word. Continue giving Team A definitions until some team member makes an incorrect response. An incorrect response sends the game back to the jumbled-word face off, this time with students 2A and 2B. Instead of repeating giving definitions to the first few students of each team, continue with the student after the one who gave the last incorrect response on the team. For example, if Team B wins the jumbled-word face-off, and student 5B gave the last incorrect answer for Team B, you would start this round of definition questions with student 6B, and so on. The team with the most points wins!

7. Have students write a story in which they correctly use as many vocabulary words as possible. Have students read their compositions orally! Post the most original compositions on your bulletin board!

LESSON TWENTY-ONE

Objective

To review the main ideas and events in *Walk Two Moons*

Activity #1

Choose one of the following review games/activities and spend your class time as directed there.

1. Ask the class to make up a unit test for *Walk Two Moons*. The test should have 4 sections: matching, true/false, short answer, and essay. Students may use 1/2 period to make the test and then swap papers and use the other 1/2 class period to take a test a classmate has devised. (open book) You may want to use the unit test included in this packet or take questions from the students' unit tests to formulate your own test.

2. Take 1/2 period for students to make up true and false questions (including the answers). Collect the papers and divide the class into two teams. Draw a big tic-tac-toe board on the chalk board. Make one team X and one team O. Ask questions to each side, giving each student one turn. If the question is answered correctly, that students' team's letter (X or O) is placed in the box. If the answer is incorrect, no letter is placed in the box. The object is to get three in a row like tic-tac-toe. You may want to keep track of the number of games won for each team.

3. Take 1/2 period for students to make up questions (true/false and short answer). Collect the questions. Divide the class into two teams. You'll alternate asking questions to individual members of teams A & B (like in a spelling bee). The question keeps going from A to B until it is correctly answered, then a new question is asked. A correct answer does not allow the team to get another question. Correct answers are +2 points; incorrect answers are -1 point.

4. Have students pair up and quiz each other from their study guides and class notes.

5. Give students a *Walk Two Moons* crossword puzzle to complete.

6. Divide your class into two teams. Use *Walk Two Moons* crossword words with their letters jumbled as a word list. Student 1 from Team A faces off against Student 1 from Team B. You write the first jumbled word on the board. The first student (1A or 1B) to unscramble the word wins the chance for his/her team to score points. If 1A wins the jumble, go to student 2A and give him/her a clue. He/she must give you the correct word which matches that clue. If he/she does, Team A scores a point, and you give student 3A a clue for which you expect another correct response. Continue giving Team A clues until some team member makes an incorrect response. An incorrect response sends the game back to the jumbled-word face off, this time with students 2A and 2B. Instead of repeating giving clues to the first few students of each team, continue with the student after the one who gave the last incorrect response on the team. For example, if Team B wins the jumbled-word face-off, and student 5B gave the last incorrect answer for Team B, you would start this round of clue questions with student 6B, and so on. The team with the most points wins!

Review Games Page 2

8. Play What's My Line?. This is similar to the old television show. Students assume the roles of different characters from the epic. One student gives clues to the class, or to a panel of contestants. The contestants try to guess the identity of the guest. Students may enjoy assisting you in creating rules and procedures for the game.

9. Play Jeopardy. Divide the class into two groups. Assign each group a category or book from the epic and have them devise answers for that category. Play the game according to the television show procedures.

10. Play Drawing in the Details. This is similar to Pictionary. Divide students into teams. A student from one team draws a scene from the epic. (You may want to specify the Book or section.) Drawings should be kept simple, to keep the pace lively. Students in the opposing team locate the scene in their books and read it aloud. If they are incorrect, the illustrator's team has a chance to guess. Involve students in setting up a scoring system and any other necessary rules.

UNIT TESTS

SHORT ANSWER UNIT TEST 1 *Walk Two Moons*

I. Short Answer

1. Who was Sal locked in a car with for six days?

2. Write down **one** of the messages left on Phoebe's front step.

3. "We had absolutely no idea all the trouble they were going to cause." To what does this statement refer?

4. What did Sal write about in her journal for Mr. Birkway?

5. What happened the night Sal fell from the oak tree?

6. What did Sal find unsettling about Mrs. Partridge?

7. What made Mr. Birkway regret sharing the journals?

8. When Mrs. Winterbottom returned home, what was different about her?

9. Who survived the bus crash?

SHORT ANSWER UNIT TEST 1 *Walk Two Moons* Page 2

II. Quotations. Explain the importance or significance of each of the following quotations.

1. "Don't judge a man until you've walked two moons in his moccasins." Chapter 9

2. "A person isn't a bird. You can't cage a person." Chapter 22

3. "You can't keep the birds of sadness from flying over your head, but you can keep them from nesting in your hair." Chapter 24

4. "Once, before she left, my mother said that if you visualize something happening, you can make it happen." Chapter 30

5. "We never know the worth of water, until the well is dry." Chapter 31

SHORT ANSWER UNIT TEST 1 *Walk Two Moons*   Page 3

III. Essay

Sal experienced a great deal on her trip to Idaho. Describe one of the life lessons she learned along the way and how she learned it.

SHORT ANSWER UNIT TEST 1 *Walk Two Moons* Page 4

IV. Vocabulary
Listen to the vocabulary words, and write them down. Then go back and write down the definition for each word.

1.

2.

3.

4.

5.

6.

7.

8.

9.

10.

ANSWER KEY SHORT ANSWER UNIT TEST 1 *Walk Two Moons*

I. Short Answer

1. Who was Sal locked in a car with for six days?
    She was locked in a car with her grandparents.

2. Write down **one** of the messages left on Phoebe's front step.
    "Don't judge a man until you've walked two moons in his moccasins."
    "Everyone has his own agenda."
    "In the course of a lifetime, what does it matter."
    "You can't keep the birds of sadness from flying over your head, but you can keep them from nesting in your head."

3. "We had absolutely no idea all the trouble they were going to cause." To what did this statement refer?
    This statement referred to the journals Mr. Birkway collected.

4. What did Sal write about in her journal for Mr. Birkway?
    She wrote about the blackberry kiss, a memory associated with her mother.

5. What happened the night Sal fell from the oak tree?
    Sal's mother gave birth, but the baby was stillborn.

6. What did Sal find unsettling about Mrs. Partridge?
    Despite being blind, Mrs. Partridge could see everything Phoebe was doing.

7. What made Mr. Birkway regret sharing the journals?
    He read a passage suggesting his sister, Mrs. Cadaver, was a murderer.

8. When Mrs. Winterbottom returned home, what was different about her?
    Her hair was short and stylish, and she had on makeup. She was also wearing jeans and a T – shirt.

9. Who survived the bus crash?
    Mrs. Cadaver

ANSWER KEY SHORT ANSWER TEST 1 *Walk Two Moons*

II. Quotations: Explain the importance or significance of each of the following quotations.

ANSWERS WILL VARY DEPENDING ON YOUR CLASS DISCUSSIONS AND THE LEVEL OF YOUR CLASS.

III. ESSAY
Sal experienced a great deal on her trip to Idaho. Describe one of the life lessons she learned along the way.

ANSWERS WILL VARY DEPENDING ON YOUR CLASS DISCUSSIONS AND THE LEVEL OF YOUR CLASS.

IV. Vocabulary
Choose 10 of the vocabulary words. Read them orally for students to write down.

SHORT ANSWER UNIT TEST 2 *Walk Two Moons*

I. Short Answer

1. Write down **one** of the messages left on Phoebe's front step.

2. What happened to Gram while she was wading in the Missouri River?

3. "We had absolutely no idea all the trouble they were going to cause." To what does this statement refer?

4. Why did Sal's mother leave?

5. Why did Sal like Phoebe?

6. Who did Sal recognize in Sergeant Bickle's photograph?

7. What was Mrs. Winterbottom scared to tell her husband?

8. Where did the sheriff take Sal?

SHORT ANSWER UNIT TEST 2 *Walk Two Moons* Page 2

II. Quotations. Explain the importance or significance of each of the following quotations.

1. "What I have since realized is that if people expect you to be brave, sometimes you pretend that you are, even when you are frightened down to your very bones." Chapter 3

2. "Everyone has his own agenda." Chapter 11

3. "Sal, you're trying to catch fish in the air." Chapter 19

4. "You can't keep the birds of sadness from flying over your head, but you can keep them from nesting in your hair." Chapter 24

5. "We never know the worth of water, until the well is dry." Chapter 31

SHORT ANSWER UNIT TEST 2 *Walk Two Moons* Page 3

III. Essay

Sal and her grandparents visit many places on their way to Idaho. Name two places and tell how each of these scenes enhances the story.

SHORT ANSWER UNIT TEST 2 *Walk Two Moons* Page 4

IV. Vocabulary
Listen to the vocabulary words, and write them down. Then go back and write down the definition for each word.

1.

2.

3.

4.

5.

6.

7.

8.

9.

10

ANSWER KEY SHORT ANSWER UNIT TEST 2 *Walk Two Moons*

I. Short Answer

1. Write down **one** of the messages left on Phoebe's front step.
   "Don't judge a man until you've walked two moons in his moccasins."
   "Everyone has his own agenda."
   "In the course of a lifetime, what does it matter."
   "You can't keep the birds of sadness from flying over your head, but you can keep them from nesting in your head."

2. What happened to Gram while she was wading in the Missouri River?
   A water moccasin bit her.

3. "We had absolutely no idea all the trouble they were going to cause." To what does this statement refer?
   This statement refers to the journals Mr. Birkway collected.

4. Why did Sal's mother leave?
   She wanted to clear her head and "to clear her heart of all the bad things." She also wanted to learn about what she was on her own.

5. Why did Sal like Phoebe?
   In spite of Phoebe's annoying ways, Sal liked Phoebe and was drawn to her. Sal felt that Phoebe "acted out the way I sometimes felt."

6. Who did Sal recognize in Sergeant Bickle's photograph?
   She recognized the lunatic.

7. What was Mrs. Winterbottom scared to tell her husband?
   She was scared to tell him that Mike Bickle was her son.

9. Where did the sheriff take Sal?
   He took her to her mother's grave.

ANSWER KEY SHORT ANSWER TEST 2 *Walk Two Moons*

II. Quotations: Explain the importance or significance of each of the following quotations.

ANSWERS WILL VARY DEPENDING ON YOUR CLASS DISCUSSIONS AND THE LEVEL OF YOUR CLASS.

III. ESSAY
Sal and her grandparents visit many places on their way to Idaho. How do some of the places they visit enhance the story?

ANSWERS WILL VARY DEPENDING ON YOUR CLASS DISCUSSIONS AND THE LEVEL OF YOUR CLASS.

IV. Vocabulary
Choose 10 of the vocabulary words. Read them orally for students to write down.

ADVANCED SHORT ANSWER UNIT TEST *Walk Two Moons*

I. Short answer

1. In what ways did telling the story of Phoebe help Sal?

2. What did Phoebe gain from Sal's friendship?

3. How did the myth of Pandora's box tie into the story?

4. How does Sal change from the beginning of the book to the end of the book?

5. Compare and contrast Phoebe and Sal.

6. Explain how the author's use of dialect and idioms provides voice to the characters.

ADVANCED SHORT ANSWER TEST *Walk Two Moons* Page 2

II. Quotations. Explain the importance of significance of each of the following quotations.

1. "I realized that the story of Phoebe was like the plaster wall in our old house in Bybanks, Kentucky." Chapter 1

2. "Being a mother is like trying to hold a wolf by the ears." Chapter 10

3. "Sal, you're trying to catch fish in the air." Chapter 19

4. "Sometimes you know in your heart you love someone, but you have to go away before your head can figure it out." Chapter 24

5. "I decided that bravery is looking Pandora's box full in the eye as best you can, and then turning to the other box, the one with the smoothbeautiful folds: . . ." Chapter 44

ADVANCED SHORT ANSWER UNIT TEST *Walk Two Moons* Page 3

III. Essay

Describe the significance of Sal's relationship to her grandparents. Compare and contrast it to Sal's relationship with her father.

ADVANCED SHORT ANSWER UNIT TEST *Walk Two Moons* Page 4

IV. Vocabulary

Listen to the vocabulary words, and write them down. Then go back and write a paragraph about *Walk Two Moons* using at least 8 of the words from the list.

MULTIPLE CHOICE UNIT TEST 1 – *Walk Two Moons*

I. Matching Unit Words.   Write the letter of the correct description next to each unit word or phrase.

____ 1.   Old Faithful   A.   Gramps often referred to Gram as _____.

____ 2.   Huzza Huzza   B.   Sal's teacher

____ 3.   Bybanks, Kentucky   C.   The person who left the messages

____ 4.   Salamanca Tree Hiddle   D.   Mrs. Winterbottom's son

____ 5.   Chanhassen   E.   A phrase Gram often uses

____ 6.   Gooseberry   F.   The lunatic's father

____ 7.   Worrier   G.   Where "Old Faithful" can be found

____ 8.   Mr. Birkway   H.   Sal hears a birdsong coming from _____.

____ 9.   An aspen tree   I.   Sal's mother said she would return_____.

____ 10. Margaret Cadaver   J.   Ben gives Sal _____.

____ 11. Before the tulips bloom   K.   Sacred Land of the Sioux Indians

____ 12. Mrs. Partridge   L.   Sal's real name

____ 13. Sargeant Bickle   M.   Sal's mother's real name

____ 14. Mike Bickle   N.   Where Sal lived most of her thirteen years

____ 15. Ben Finney   O.   She worked at Rocky's Rubber

____ 16. A chicken   P.   He kisses Sal

____ 17. The Black Hills   Q.   Phoebe thinks this person is a murderer

____ 18. Yellowstone National Park   R.   Something Gram waited her whole life to see

____ 19. Mrs. Winterbottom   S.   Phoebe was a champion _____.

____ 20. Sharon Creech   T.   Author of *Walk Two Moons*

MULTIPLE CHOICE UNIT TEST 1 *Walk Two Moons* Page 2

II. Multiple Choice

1. Who was Sal locked in a car with for six days?
    a. Phoebe Winterbottom
    b. Her grandparents
    c. Her father
    d. Margaret Cadaver

2. Who was Mrs. Partridge?
    a. Sal's teacher
    b. Sal's aunt
    c. Phoebe Winterbottom's grandmother
    d. Margaret Cadaver's mother

3. Which is an example of how Sal's grandparents got into trouble?
    a. At the airport, they got into trouble for failing to show proper identification.
    b. In Washington D.C., they were arrested for stealing the back tires off a senator's car.
    c. In Philadelphia, they got into trouble for touching famous works of art.
    d. They got into trouble for bringing their pets into a restaurant.

4. What whispering words did Sal hear on the way to Idaho?
    a. "Be careful, don't get hurt."
    b. "Rush, hurry, rush."
    c. "Remember, I love you."
    d. "Don't worry. You'll find out the truth."

5. Which term did Sal's mother and Gram not like?
    a. Native American
    b. Peace Pipe
    c. Gooseberry
    d. Indian Joe

6. "We had absolutely no idea all the trouble they were going to cause." To what does this statement refer?
    a. The peace pipes Gramps purchased
    b. The cartoons Ben drew
    c. The journals Mr. Birkway collected
    d. The articles in the newspaper about Mrs. Cadaver

7. Who was Tom Fleet?
    a. Mr. Hiddle's best friend
    b. A man who wanted to meet Phoebe because he claimed to know the lunatic
    c. A boy who initially threatened Sal and her grandparents but who helped save Gram's life
    d. Mrs. Cadaver's nightshift co-worker

MULTIPLE CHOICE UNIT TEST 1 *Walk Two Moons* Page 3

Matching (cont.)

8. What did Sal write about in her journal for Mr. Birkway?
    a. Her beloved pet rabbit
    b. An Indian story about the passing of the seasons
    c. The sad journey to Euclid, Ohio
    d. The blackberry kiss, a memory associated with her mother

9. Who found Sal after she fell from an oak tree?
    a. Her mother
    b. Her father
    c. Gramps
    d. Gram

10. When Sal said, "This ain't your marriage bed.", how did Gramps reply?"
    a. "But is sure feels like it."
    b. "It is as hard as a rock."
    c. "But it will have to do."
    d. "Ours is back home waiting for us."

MULTIPLE CHOICE UNIT TEST 1 *Walk Two Moons* Page 4

III. Vocabulary. Match the vocabulary words to their dictionary definitions.

____ 1. Bountiful A. Legal

____ 2. Noble B. Taken or held prisoner

____ 3. Berserk C. The tendency to expect the best outcome

____ 4. Legitimate D. To comfort

____ 5. Miscellaneous E. A ruining or being ruined

____ 6. Embedded F. Bold resistance to authority

____ 7. Colossal G. A dead body

____ 8. Captive H. Showing high moral qualities

____ 9. Elaborate I. Very wicked or cruel

____ 10. Console J. Plentiful

____ 11. Diabolic K. To add more details

____ 12. Ruination L. Varied; mixed

____ 13. Malinger M. Set or fixed firmly

____ 14. Sullen N. Gloomy; dismal

____ 15. Defiance O. To pretend to be ill to escape work

____ 16. Omnipotent P. Not easily convinced or persuaded

____ 17. Skeptical Q. Having unlimited power

____ 18. Cadaver R. Huge; gigantic

____ 19. Optimistic S. In a state of violent or destructive rage or frenzy

____ 20. Pandemonium T. Wild disorder, noise, or confusion

MULTIPLE CHOICE TEST 1 *Walk Two Moons* Page 5

IV. Composition

What did Mrs. Winterbottom mean when she asked, "Do you think I lead a tiny life?" What type of life do you think she led prior to meeting her son? How do you think her life will change?

ANSWER SHEET MULTIPLE CHOICE UNIT TEST 1 *Walk Two Moons*

I. Matching	II. Multiple Choice	IV. Vocabulary
1. ___	1. ___	1. ___
2. ___	2. ___	2. ___
3. ___	3. ___	3. ___
4. ___	4. ___	4. ___
5. ___	5. ___	5. ___
6. ___	6. ___	6. ___
7. ___	7. ___	7. ___
8. ___	8. ___	8. ___
9. ___	9. ___	9. ___
10. ___	10. ___	10. ___
11. ___		11. ___
12. ___		12. ___
13. ___		13. ___
14. ___		14. ___
15. ___		15. ___
16. ___		16. ___
17. ___		17. ___
18. ___		18. ___
19. ___		19. ___
20. ___		20. ___

ANSWER KEY MULTIPLE CHOICE UNIT TEST 1 *Walk Two Moons*

I. Matching	II. Multiple Choice	III. Vocabulary
1. R	1. B	1. J
2. E	2. D	2. H
3. N	3. B	3. S
4. L	4. B	4. A
5. M	5. A	5. L
6. A	6. C	6. M
7. S	7. C	7. R
8. B	8. D	8. B
9. H	9. A	9. K
10. Q	10. C	10. D
11. I		11. I
12. C		12. E
13. F		13. O
14. D		14. N
15. P		15. F
16. J		16. Q
17. K		17. P
18. G		18. G
19. O		19. C
20. T		20. T

MULTIPLE CHOICE UNIT TEST 2 – *Walk Two Moons*

I. Matching Unit Words. Write the letter of the correct description next to each unit word or phrase.

____ 1.	Huzza Huzza	A.	The lunatic's father
____ 2.	The Black Hills	B.	Sal wrote in her journal about _____.
____ 3.	Worrier	C.	Phoebe thinks this person is a murderer.
____ 4.	Pandora	D.	Mrs. Winterbottom's son
____ 5.	Mrs. Partridge	E.	He kisses Sal
____ 6.	Mrs. Winterbottom	F.	Gramps often referred to Gram as _____.
____ 7.	Bybanks, Kentucky	G.	Where "Old Faithful" can be found
____ 8.	A blackberry kiss	H.	Sal hears a birdsong coming from _____.
____ 9.	A chicken	I.	Gram got bit by _____.
____ 10.	Margaret Cadaver	J.	Ben gives Sal _____.
____ 11.	A water moccasin	K.	Sacred Land of the Sioux Indians
____ 12.	Mr. Birkway	L.	Phoebe did a report on _____.
____ 13.	Sargeant Bickle	M.	Margaret Cadaver's brother
____ 14.	Sharon Creech	N.	Where Sal lived most of her thirteen years
____ 15.	Ben Finney	O.	She worked at Rocky's Rubber
____ 16.	An aspen tree	P.	A phrase Gram often uses
____ 17.	Old Faithful	Q.	The person who left the messages
____ 18.	Yellowstone National Park	R.	Something Gram waited her whole life to see
____ 19.	Gooseberry	S.	Phoebe was a champion _____.
____ 20.	Mike Bickle	T.	Author of *Walk Two Moons*

MULTIPLE CHOICE UNIT TEST 2 *Walk Two Moons* Page 2

II. Multiple Choice

1. Once Sal decided to go on the trip, she prayed she would be in Idaho by when?
    a. She prayed she would be in Idaho before it started to snow.
    b. She prayed she would be in Idaho before the start of the school year.
    c. She prayed she would be in Idaho by her mother's birthday.
    d. She prayed she would be in Idaho before she turned fourteen.

2. Which is an example of how Sal's grandparents got into trouble?
    a. At the airport, they got into trouble for failing to show proper identification.
    b. In Washington D.C., they were arrested for stealing the back tires off a senator's car.
    c. In Philadelphia, they got into trouble for touching famous works of art.
    d. They got into trouble for bringing their pets into a restaurant.

3. "We had absolutely no idea all the trouble they were going to cause." To what does this statement refer?
    a. The peace pipes Gramps purchased
    b. The cartoons Ben drew
    c. The journals Mr. Birkway collected
    d. The articles in the newspaper about Mrs. Cadaver

4. From what type of tree did Sal hear the beautiful birdsong coming?
    a. An aspen tree
    b. A sugar maple tree
    c. An oak tree
    d. A palm tree

5. Phoebe told her classmates that her mother was away in what city?
    a. Tokyo
    b. London
    c. Chicago
    d. Paris

6. What was the only good thing in Pandora's box?
    a. Love
    b. Friendship
    c. Hope
    d. Family

MULTIPLE CHOICE UNIT TEST 2 *Walk Two Moons* Page 3

II. Multiple Choice (Continued)

7. Who said, "Maybe dying should be normal and terrible."
    a. Ben
    b. Sal
    c. Mr. Hiddle
    d. Gram

8. Who did Sal recognize in Sergeant Bickle's photograph?
    a. Ben
    b. Mrs. Winterbottom
    c. Mrs. Bickle
    d. The lunatic

9. When Mrs. Winterbottom returned home, what was different about her?
    a. Her hair was short and stylish, and she had on makeup.
    b. She was tired and appeared to have lost weight.
    c. She was less willing to do everything for her children and husband.
    d. She quit her old job and enrolled in college to become a lawyer.

10. What did it take Sal four hours to do?
    a. It took her four hours to learn how to drive a car.
    b. It took her four hours to convince Gramps to drive back to Ohio.
    c. It took her four hours to drive one hundred miles to the top of Lewiston Hill.
    d. It took her four hours to work up the courage to leave Coeur D'Alene.

MULTIPLE CHOICE UNIT TEST 2 *Walk Two Moons* Page 4

III. Vocabulary. Match the vocabulary words to their dictionary definitions.

    ____ 1. Rhododendron   A. Having or showing religious devotion

    ____ 2. Crucial   B. Taken or held prisoner

    ____ 3. Berserk   C. Challenging; daring

    ____ 4. Pious   D. To comfort

    ____ 5. Intriguing   E. An impelling force

    ____ 6. Dissuade   F. Quarrelsome

    ____ 7. Colossal   G. A dead body

    ____ 8. Captive   H. Of supreme importance

    ____ 9. Elaborate   I. Persuade against (an action)

    ____ 10. Console   J. A shrub with showy flowers of pink, white, or purple

    ____ 11. Diabolic   K. To add more details

    ____ 12. Impulse   L. Exciting interest or curiosity

    ____ 13. Malinger   M. Extremely evil

    ____ 14. Sullen   N. Gloomy; dismal

    ____ 15. Cantankerous   O. To pretend to be ill to escape work

    ____ 16. Omnipotent   P. Judgments without all the evidence

    ____ 17. Prejudgments   Q. Having unlimited power

    ____ 18. Cadaver   R. Huge; gigantic

    ____ 19. Defying   S. In a state of violent or destructive rage or frenzy

    ____ 20. Pandemonium   T. Wild disorder, noise, or confusion

IV. Essay

Compare and contrast Sal's mother to Phoebe's mother. Think about their relationships with family members, their backgrounds, their interests, and their personal problems.

ANSWER SHEET MULTIPLE CHOICE UNIT TEST 2 *Walk Two Moons*

I. Matching	II. Multiple Choice	IV. Vocabulary
1. ___	1. ___	1. ___
2. ___	2. ___	2. ___
3. ___	3. ___	3. ___
4. ___	4. ___	4. ___
5. ___	5. ___	5. ___
6. ___	6. ___	6. ___
7. ___	7. ___	7. ___
8. ___	8. ___	8. ___
9. ___	9. ___	9. ___
10. ___	10. ___	10. ___
11. ___		11. ___
12. ___		12. ___
13. ___		13. ___
14. ___		14. ___
15. ___		15. ___
16. ___		16. ___
17. ___		17. ___
18. ___		18. ___
19. ___		19. ___
20. ___		20. ___

ANSWER KEY MULTIPLE CHOICE UNIT TEST 2 *Walk Two Moons*

I. Matching	II. Multiple Choice	III. Vocabulary
1. P	1. C	1. J
2. K	2. B	2. H
3. S	3. C	3. S
4. L	4. A	4. A
5. Q	5. B	5. L
6. O	6. C	6. I
7. N	7. A	7. R
8. B	8. D	8. B
9. J	9. A	9. K
10. C	10. C	10. D
11. I		11. M
12. M		12. E
13. A		13. O
14. T		14. N
15. E		15. F
16. H		16. Q
17. R		17. P
18. G		18. G
19. F		19. C
20. D		20. T

UNIT RESOURCE MATERIALS

BULLETIN BOARD IDEAS – *Walk Two Moons*

1. Save one corner of the board for the best of students' *Walk Two Moons* writing assignments.

2. Take one of the word search puzzles and copy it over in a large size on the bulletin board. Write the clue words to find to one side. Invite students prior to and after class to find the words and circle them on the bulletin board.

3. Write several of the most significant quotations from the book onto the board on brightly colored paper.

4. Make a bulletin board listing the vocabulary words for this unit. As you complete sections of the novel and discuss the vocabulary for each section, write the definitions on the bulletin board. (If your board is one students face frequently, it will help them learn the words.)

5. Have students write down and illustrate their favorite similes from the book.

6. Display photographs of the places Sal visited on her journey west.

7. Have students research a few poems written by Longfellow and e. e. cummings. Display their favorites lines and/or stanzas.

8. Display a list of Sharon Creech's other books. Include a brief synopsis of each book.

9. Display each group's fictional journal entries and maps.

10. Obtain a copy of the optical illusion/perception exercise mentioned in chapter 32 (two faces or the vase). Construct a bar graph that illustrates how many students saw the woman compared to how many saw the vase. Include other examples such as the famous old woman/young woman image.

EXTRA ACTIVITIES – *Walk Two Moons*

One of the difficulties in teaching a novel is that all students don't read at the same speed. One student who likes to read may take the book home and finish it in a day or two. Sometimes a few students finish the in-class assignments early. The problem, then, is finding suitable extra activities for students.

One thing that seems to help is to keep a little library in the classroom. For this unit on *Walk Two Moons*, you might check out from the school library poems by Longfellow and e. e. cummings, mythology and legends collections, national park guides, historical fiction selections such as *Pocahontas* by Joseph Bruchac, and other books by Marion Creech.

Other things you may keep on hand are puzzles. This manual includes some relating directly to *Walk Two Moons* for you. Feel free to duplicate them for your students to use.

Some students may like to draw. You might devise a contest or allow some extra-credit grade for students who draw characters or scenes from *Walk Two Moons*. Note, too, that if the students do not want to keep their drawings you may pick up some extra bulletin board materials this way. If you have a contest and you supply the prize (a CD or something like that perhaps), you could, possibly, make the drawing itself a non-returnable entry fee.

The pages which follow contain games, puzzles and worksheets. The keys, when appropriate, immediately follow the puzzle or worksheet. There are two main groups of activities: one group for the unit; that is, generally relating to *Walk Two Moons* text, and another group of activities related strictly to *Walk Two Moons* vocabulary.

Directions for these games, puzzles and worksheets are self-explanatory. The object here is to provide you with extra materials you may use in any way you choose.

MORE ACTIVITIES – *Walk Two Moons*

1. Have students work together to make a time line chronology of the events in the story. Take a large piece of construction paper and on one wall (or however you can physically arrange it in your room) and make the events of the story along it. Students may want to add drawings or cut-out pictures to represent the events (as well as a written statement).

2. Have students design a book cover (front and back and inside flaps) for *Walk Two Moons*.

3. Have students design a bulletin board (ready to be put up; not just sketched) for *Walk Two Moons*.

4. Have students group the chapters together to show the larger structure of the novel. Have them explain why they chose the divisions they made.

5. Have students choose one chapter of the book (with sufficient dialogue) to rewrite as a play. In conjunction with this assignment, have students write a composition explaining the difficulties they encountered in changing from one written form to another.

6. Initiate a discussion of American Indian representation. Use the following questions to guide the discussion: How are American Indians represented today? What objects and practices do we associated with American Indian culture? What are some customs and traditions? Which term should be used, American Indian or Native American?

7. Obtain a copy of the Native American Graves Protection and Repatriation Act of 1990 (NAGRPA). Highlight sections of the act that detail how American Indian cultural artifacts can be returned (from museums) to various tribes. Visit websites such as the National Museum of the American Indian and the Museum of Anthropology, Vancouver, British Columbia as resources.

8. Interested students may way wish to write the first chapter of the *Walk Two Moons* sequel.

9. Use the book as a springboard to a mini-unit on mythology. Include selections from Greek, Roman, and Native American mythology.

Walk Two Moons Word List

No.	Word	Clue/Definition
1.	AGENDA	One message said," Everyone has his own ___."
2.	BED	"This ain't our marriage ___, but it will do."
3.	BEN	He drew a picture of Sal as a lizard-like creature with long, black hair.
4.	BICKLE	Police sergeant Phoebe talks to about her missing mother
5.	BIRKWAY	Mrs. Partridge's son and Mrs. Cadaver's twin brother
6.	BIRTHDAY	Sal wanted to be in Lewiston by her mother's.
7.	BUS	It skidded off the road, killing Sal's mother.
8.	CADAVER	Phoebe thinks she murdered her husband.
9.	CAR	Sal was locked in one with her grandparents for 6 days.
10.	CHICKEN	Ben gave one to Sal.
11.	CREECH	Author
12.	DRUNK	A ___ driver rammed into Mr. Cadaver's car.
13.	FAITHFUL	Gram always wanted to see Old ___.
14.	FINNEYS	Phoebe eats dinner at this odd family's house.
15.	FIREPLACE	Sal's father uncovered one when he learned Sal's mother wasn't coming home.
16.	GRAVE	The sheriff took Sal to her mother's.
17.	HOPE	The only good thing in Pandora's box
18.	HOSPITAL	Gram had to go there
19.	HUZZA	Gram's saying: _____ _____ (same word twice)
20.	IDAHO	The trip destination
21.	INDIANS	Gram dances with them.
22.	JOURNALS	We had no idea all the trouble they were going to cause.
23.	JUDGE	"Don't ___ a man until you've walked two moons in his moccasins."
24.	LUNATIC	Name the girls give the strange boy who came to Phoebe's house
25.	MICHIGAN	Gram put her feet into this lake.
26.	MIKE	The Lunatic
27.	MOCCASIN	A water ___ bit Gram.
28.	MOONS	Walk Two ___
29.	NORMAL	Maybe dying should be ___ and terrible, according to Ben.
30.	NOTE	Mrs. Winterbottom leaves one for Mr. Winterbottom saying she had to go away.
31.	PARTRIDGE	Even though she is blind, she can see everything Phoebe is doing.
32.	PHOEBE	Sal entertained her grandparents with stories about her.
33.	PIPE	It's for remembering with: peace ___
34.	PORCH	Place where the mysterious messages were left
35.	PRUDENCE	Phoebe's sister
36.	RUSH	One of the whispering words Sal heard on her trip
37.	SACRIFICES	According to Phoebe's mother, in life you have to make some ___.
38.	SALAMANCA	Sal's whole first name
39.	SIMPLE	Word Sal used to describe her father
40.	SIOUX	The Black Hills are sacred to them.
41.	SON	Mike Bickle's relationship to Mrs. Winterbottom
42.	STILLBORN	Condition of Sal's mother's baby
43.	TIRES	Sal's grandparents got arrested for stealing these in Washington D.C.
44.	TOM	He helped save Gram's life: ___ Fleet
45.	TULIPS	Sal's mother's good-bye letter says she will return before they bloom.

WORD SEARCH Walk Two Moons

```
Y F C L T G H Z I F G Q H W X W M W X B
G I V F R Y F Z N X D U L N V N O B W F
Y N J A V W D S D T Z N S A P Z O I N H
M N V Z T C P F I Z G M M G G J N R B X
Z E B E P I P S A C R I F I C E S K L Y
B Y Q F L T R J N I Y W B H J O U W A S
Q S P U R A V E S C T R B C N M B A T Y
B X T W P N C N S Q A H S I O U X Y I C
C S G X D U P H V C N D F M D R W G P H
T E A W S L O J I F L N A U L L F M S G
B T M L H T R U B C K S Y V L S W J O Q
N O R M A L C D G E K H O P E B E O H P
S N F K O M H G G Z D E Z R L R N U S J
X P C Y A C A E V S N S N G F M B R I V
E R Z R G H C N D T M Y Y D I D I N M X
Q U K W E F V A C Z E G D I R T R A P N
H D S K N E Z J S A F Y L P E I T L L Y
M E P H D N C G B I V H T N P D H S E X
L N K M A C D H V J N L O P L A D N Y X
J C B E N D R U N K C Z M D A H A Q D V
L E W M G B D Z K V Y I S B C O Y C T Y
B I C K L E J J K F K F M W E K G F Z S
S T I L L B O R N E L L N Q P X P C Q T
```

AGENDA	GRAVE	PARTRIDGE
BED	HOPE	PHOEBE
BEN	HOSPITAL	PIPE
BICKLE	HUZZA	PORCH
BIRKWAY	IDAHO	PRUDENCE
BIRTHDAY	INDIANS	RUSH
BUS	JOURNALS	SACRIFICES
CADAVER	JUDGE	SALAMANCA
CAR	LUNATIC	SIMPLE
CHICKEN	MICHIGAN	SIOUX
CREECH	MIKE	SON
DRUNK	MOCCASIN	STILLBORN
FAITHFUL	MOONS	TIRES
FINNEYS	NORMAL	TOM
FIREPLACE	NOTE	TULIPS

WORD SEARCH ANSWER KEY Walk Two Moons

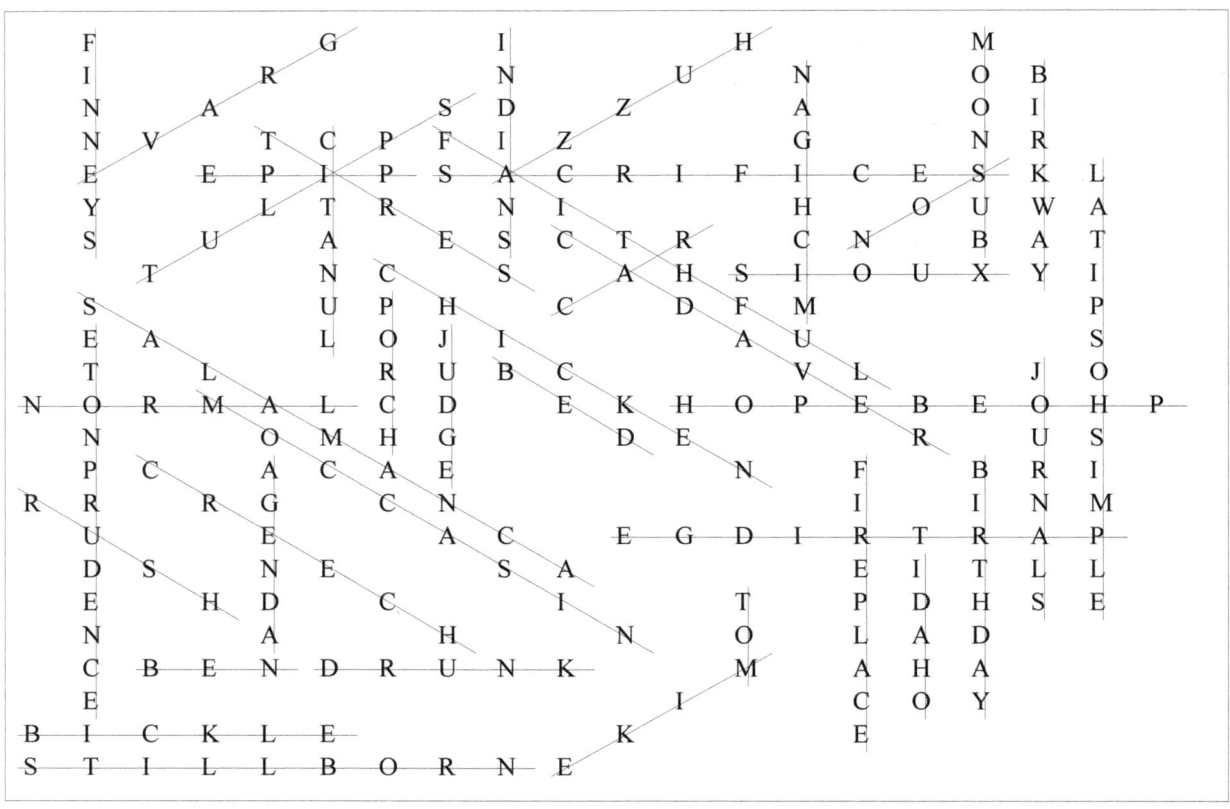

AGENDA	GRAVE	PARTRIDGE
BED	HOPE	PHOEBE
BEN	HOSPITAL	PIPE
BICKLE	HUZZA	PORCH
BIRKWAY	IDAHO	PRUDENCE
BIRTHDAY	INDIANS	RUSH
BUS	JOURNALS	SACRIFICES
CADAVER	JUDGE	SALAMANCA
CAR	LUNATIC	SIMPLE
CHICKEN	MICHIGAN	SIOUX
CREECH	MIKE	SON
DRUNK	MOCCASIN	STILLBORN
FAITHFUL	MOONS	TIRES
FINNEYS	NORMAL	TOM
FIREPLACE	NOTE	TULIPS

CROSSWORD Walk Two Moons

Across

1. He drew a picture of Sal as a lizard-like creature with long, black hair.
3. It skidded off the road, killing Sal's mother.
4. Sal was locked in one with her grandparents for 6 days.
6. Sal's grandparents got arrested for stealing these in Washington D.C.
8. One of the whispering words Sal heard on her trip
10. A ___ driver rammed into Mr. Cadaver's car.
11. Ben gave one to Sal.
12. This ain't our marriage ___, but it will do.
13. The sheriff took Sal to her mother's.
14. Phoebe eats dinner at this odd family's house.
18. One message said, "Everyone has his own ___."
19. We had no idea all the trouble they were going to cause.

Down

1. Police sergeant Phoebe talks to about her missing mother
2. Mrs. Winterbottom leaves one for Mr. Winterbottom saying she had to go away.
3. Sal wanted to be in Lewiston by her mother's.
4. Phoebe thinks she murdered her husband.
5. Author
7. According to Phoebe's mother, in life you have to make some ___.
9. The only good thing in Pandora's box
12. Mrs. Partridge's son and Mrs. Cadaver's twin brother
15. Maybe dying should be ___ and terrible, according to Ben.
16. Word Sal used to describe her father
17. The trip destination

CROSSWORD ANSWER KEY Walk Two Moons

			1 B	2 N		3 B	U	S				
4 C	A	R		I	O		I			5 C		
A				C	6 T	I	R	E	7 S	8 R	U	9 H
10 D	R	U	N	K	E		T		A	E		O
A				L	11 C	H	I	C	K	E	N	P
V	12 B	E	D		D		R		C		E
E		I			A		I		H			
R	13 G	R	A	V	E		Y		F			
	K					14 F	I	15 N	N	E	Y	16 S
	W			17 I		C		O				I
	18 A	G	E	N	D	A		R				M
	Y			A		E		S				P
				H		S		M				L
			19 J	O	U	R	N	A	L	S		E

Across

1. He drew a picture of Sal as a lizard-like creature with long, black hair.
3. It skidded off the road, killing Sal's mother.
4. Sal was locked in one with her grandparents for 6 days.
6. Sal's grandparents got arrested for stealing these in Washington D.C.
8. One of the whispering words Sal heard on her trip
10. A ___ driver rammed into Mr. Cadaver's car.
11. Ben gave one to Sal.
12. This ain't our marriage ___, but it will do.
13. The sheriff took Sal to her mother's.
14. Phoebe eats dinner at this odd family's house.
18. One message said, "Everyone has his own ___."
19. We had no idea all the trouble they were going to cause.

Down

1. Police sergeant Phoebe talks to about her missing mother
2. Mrs. Winterbottom leaves one for Mr. Winterbottom saying she had to go away.
3. Sal wanted to be in Lewiston by her mother's.
4. Phoebe thinks she murdered her husband.
5. Author
7. According to Phoebe's mother, in life you have to make some ___.
9. The only good thing in Pandora's box
12. Mrs. Partridge's son and Mrs. Cadaver's twin brother
15. Maybe dying should be ___ and terrible, according to Ben.
16. Word Sal used to describe her father
17. The trip destination

MATCHING 1 Walk Two Moons

___ 1. GRAVE
___ 2. LUNATIC
___ 3. BUS
___ 4. SALAMANCA
___ 5. FIREPLACE
___ 6. TIRES
___ 7. MOCCASIN
___ 8. PARTRIDGE
___ 9. JUDGE
___ 10. SIOUX
___ 11. BIRKWAY
___ 12. SON
___ 13. NORMAL
___ 14. MICHIGAN
___ 15. FAITHFUL
___ 16. IDAHO
___ 17. HUZZA
___ 18. BED
___ 19. DRUNK
___ 20. CREECH
___ 21. CADAVER
___ 22. CHICKEN
___ 23. SACRIFICES
___ 24. MIKE
___ 25. PIPE

A. Name the girls give the strange boy who came to Phoebe's house
B. Mike Bickle's relationship to Mrs. Winterbottom
C. Phoebe thinks she murdered her husband.
D. Mrs. Partridge's son and Mrs. Cadaver's twin brother
E. Sal's whole first name
F. Gram's saying: _____ _____ (same word twice)
G. Sal's father uncovered one when he learned Sal's mother wasn't coming home.
H. Author
I. Gram always wanted to see Old ___.
J. The Black Hills are sacred to them.
K. The trip destination
L. A ___ driver rammed into Mr. Cadaver's car.
M. Even though she is blind, she can see everything Phoebe is doing.
N. Maybe dying should be ___ and terrible, according to Ben.
O. It skidded off the road, killing Sal's mother.
P. It's for remembering with: peace ___
Q. Sal's grandparents got arrested for stealing these in Washington D.C.
R. The sheriff took Sal to her mother's.
S. According to Phoebe's mother, in life you have to make some ___.
T. "Don't ___ a man until you've walked two moons in his moccasins."
U. "This ain't our marriage ___, but it will do."
V. A water ___ bit Gram.
W. Gram put her feet into this lake.
X. Ben gave one to Sal.
Y. The Lunatic

MATCHING 1 ANSWER KEY Walk Two Moons

R - 1. GRAVE
A - 2. LUNATIC
O - 3. BUS
E - 4. SALAMANCA
G - 5. FIREPLACE
Q - 6. TIRES
V - 7. MOCCASIN
M - 8. PARTRIDGE
T - 9. JUDGE
J - 10. SIOUX
D - 11. BIRKWAY
B - 12. SON
N - 13. NORMAL
W - 14. MICHIGAN
I - 15. FAITHFUL
K - 16. IDAHO
F - 17. HUZZA
U - 18. BED
L - 19. DRUNK
H - 20. CREECH
C - 21. CADAVER
X - 22. CHICKEN
S - 23. SACRIFICES
Y - 24. MIKE
P - 25. PIPE

A. Name the girls give the strange boy who came to Phoebe's house
B. Mike Bickle's relationship to Mrs. Winterbottom
C. Phoebe thinks she murdered her husband.
D. Mrs. Partridge's son and Mrs. Cadaver's twin brother
E. Sal's whole first name
F. Gram's saying: _____ _____ (same word twice)
G. Sal's father uncovered one when he learned Sal's mother wasn't coming home.
H. Author
I. Gram always wanted to see Old ___.
J. The Black Hills are sacred to them.
K. The trip destination
L. A ___ driver rammed into Mr. Cadaver's car.
M. Even though she is blind, she can see everything Phoebe is doing.
N. Maybe dying should be ___ and terrible, according to Ben.
O. It skidded off the road, killing Sal's mother.
P. It's for remembering with: peace ___
Q. Sal's grandparents got arrested for stealing these in Washington D.C.
R. The sheriff took Sal to her mother's.
S. According to Phoebe's mother, in life you have to make some ___.
T. "Don't ___ a man until you've walked two moons in his moccasins."
U. "This ain't our marriage ___, but it will do."
V. A water ___ bit Gram.
W. Gram put her feet into this lake.
X. Ben gave one to Sal.
Y. The Lunatic

MATCHING 2 Walk Two Moons

___ 1. SIMPLE   A. Gram's saying: _____ _____ (same word twice)

___ 2. TOM   B. Place where the mysterious messages were left

___ 3. SIOUX   C. Sal's mother's good-bye letter says she will return before they bloom.

___ 4. FIREPLACE   D. The sheriff took Sal to her mother's.

___ 5. PHOEBE   E. Phoebe eats dinner at this odd family's house.

___ 6. CAR   F. Sal was locked in one with her grandparents for 6 days.

___ 7. SALAMANCA   G. Police sergeant Phoebe talks to about her missing mother

___ 8. HOPE   H. The trip destination

___ 9. BED   I. Sal's father uncovered one when he learned Sal's mother wasn't coming home.

___10. STILLBORN   J. Sal's whole first name

___11. FINNEYS   K. He helped save Gram's life: ___ Fleet

___12. HUZZA   L. "This ain't our marriage ___, but it will do."

___13. HOSPITAL   M. Sal wanted to be in Lewiston by her mother's.

___14. IDAHO   N. The Lunatic

___15. PIPE   O. One of the whispering words Sal heard on her trip

___16. NORMAL   P. Condition of Sal's mother's baby

___17. MIKE   Q. Gram had to go there

___18. BICKLE   R. Phoebe thinks she murdered her husband.

___19. BIRTHDAY   S. The Black Hills are sacred to them.

___20. GRAVE   T. A water ___ bit Gram.

___21. CADAVER   U. Word Sal used to describe her father

___22. TULIPS   V. It's for remembering with: peace ___

___23. PORCH   W. Maybe dying should be ___ and terrible, according to Ben.

___24. MOCCASIN   X. The only good thing in Pandora's box

___25. RUSH   Y. Sal entertained her grandparents with stories about her.

MATCHING 2 ANSWER KEY Walk Two Moons

U - 1. SIMPLE
K - 2. TOM
S - 3. SIOUX
I - 4. FIREPLACE
Y - 5. PHOEBE
F - 6. CAR
J - 7. SALAMANCA
X - 8. HOPE
L - 9. BED
P - 10. STILLBORN
E - 11. FINNEYS
A - 12. HUZZA
Q - 13. HOSPITAL
H - 14. IDAHO
V - 15. PIPE
W - 16. NORMAL
N - 17. MIKE
G - 18. BICKLE
M - 19. BIRTHDAY
D - 20. GRAVE
R - 21. CADAVER
C - 22. TULIPS
B - 23. PORCH
T - 24. MOCCASIN
O - 25. RUSH

A. Gram's saying: _____ _____ (same word twice)
B. Place where the mysterious messages were left
C. Sal's mother's good-bye letter says she will return before they bloom.
D. The sheriff took Sal to her mother's.
E. Phoebe eats dinner at this odd family's house.
F. Sal was locked in one with her grandparents for 6 days.
G. Police sergeant Phoebe talks to about her missing mother
H. The trip destination
I. Sal's father uncovered one when he learned Sal's mother wasn't coming home.
J. Sal's whole first name
K. He helped save Gram's life: ___ Fleet
L. "This ain't our marriage ___, but it will do."
M. Sal wanted to be in Lewiston by her mother's.
N. The Lunatic
O. One of the whispering words Sal heard on her trip
P. Condition of Sal's mother's baby
Q. Gram had to go there
R. Phoebe thinks she murdered her husband.
S. The Black Hills are sacred to them.
T. A water ___ bit Gram.
U. Word Sal used to describe her father
V. It's for remembering with: peace ___
W. Maybe dying should be ___ and terrible, according to Ben.
X. The only good thing in Pandora's box
Y. Sal entertained her grandparents with stories about her.

JUGGLE LETTER Walk Two Moons

1. UTLCANI   = 1. _____
   Name the girls give the strange boy who came to Phoebe's house

2. OMT   = 2. _____
   He helped save Gram's life: ___ Fleet

3. HODIA   = 3. _____
   The trip destination

4. ASINDNI   = 4. _____
   Gram dances with them.

5. SEPLIM   = 5. _____
   Word Sal used to describe her father

6. EICBLK   = 6. _____
   Police sergeant Phoebe talks to about her missing mother

7. NIEYFNS   = 7. _____
   Phoebe eats dinner at this odd family's house.

8. NURKD   = 8. _____
   A ___ driver rammed into Mr. Cadaver's car.

9. RTIES   = 9. _____
   Sal's grandparents got arrested for stealing these in Washington D.C.

10. CREEDNUP   =10. _____
    Phoebe's sister

11. SUB   =11. _____
    It skidded off the road, killing Sal's mother.

12. IAREPLEFC   =12. _____
    Sal's father uncovered one when he learned Sal's mother wasn't coming home.

13. EHPEOB   =13. _____
    Sal entertained her grandparents with stories about her.

14. IUOXS   =14. _____
    The Black Hills are sacred to them.

15. EBD   =15. _____
    "This ain't our marriage ___, but it will do."

16. LTHUIFAF =16. _____
Gram always wanted to see Old ___.

17. SLUOJNAR =17. _____
We had no idea all the trouble they were going to cause.

18. OHCRP =18. _____
Place where the mysterious messages were left

19. MRAONL =19. _____
Maybe dying should be ___ and terrible, according to Ben.

20. PIUSTL =20. _____
Sal's mother's good-bye letter says she will return before they bloom.

21. AINHMIGC =21. _____
Gram put her feet into this lake.

22. NGDEAA =22. _____
One message said, "Everyone has his own ___."

23. ADRBTHYI =23. _____
Sal wanted to be in Lewiston by her mother's.

24. ONS =24. _____
Mike Bickle's relationship to Mrs. Winterbottom

25. SUHR =25. _____
One of the whispering words Sal heard on her trip

26. PEIP =26. _____
It's for remembering with: peace ___

27. BEN =27. _____
He drew a picture of Sal as a lizard-like creature with long, black hair.

28. EHECRC =28. _____
Author

29. CCMNSOIA =29. _____
A water ___ bit Gram.

30. KWYIRBA =30. _____
Mrs. Partridge's son and Mrs. Cadaver's twin brother

31. ETNO =31. _____
Mrs. Winterbottom leaves one for Mr. Winterbottom saying she had to go away.

32. IKME =32. _____
The Lunatic

33. ASCNLMAAA =33. _____
Sal's whole first name

34. RAVEG =34. _____
The sheriff took Sal to her mother's.

35. DJUGE =35. _____
"Don't ___ a man until you've walked two moons in his moccasins."

36. CCHEIKN =36. _____
Ben gave one to Sal.

37. EPRIRDAGT =37. _____
Even though she is blind, she can see everything Phoebe is doing.

38. RAC =38. _____
Sal was locked in one with her grandparents for 6 days.

39. ADEARVC =39. _____
Phoebe thinks she murdered her husband.

40. PLHOSATI =40. _____
Gram had to go there

41. SIIREACCFS =41. _____
According to Phoebe's mother, in life you have to make some ___.

42. OHPE =42. _____
The only good thing in Pandora's box

43. NBIRLOTLS =43. _____
Condition of Sal's mother's baby

44. AHZZU =44. _____
Gram's saying: _____ _____ (same word twice)

45. ONOMS =45. _____
Walk Two ___

JUGGLE LETTER ANSWER KEY Walk Two Moons

1. UTLCANI = 1. LUNATIC
   Name the girls give the strange boy who came to Phoebe's house

2. OMT = 2. TOM
   He helped save Gram's life: ___ Fleet

3. HODIA = 3. IDAHO
   The trip destination

4. ASINDNI = 4. INDIANS
   Gram dances with them.

5. SEPLIM = 5. SIMPLE
   Word Sal used to describe her father

6. EICBLK = 6. BICKLE
   Police sergeant Phoebe talks to about her missing mother

7. NIEYFNS = 7. FINNEYS
   Phoebe eats dinner at this odd family's house.

8. NURKD = 8. DRUNK
   A ___ driver rammed into Mr. Cadaver's car.

9. RTIES = 9. TIRES
   Sal's grandparents got arrested for stealing these in Washington D.C.

10. CREEDNUP = 10. PRUDENCE
    Phoebe's sister

11. SUB = 11. BUS
    It skidded off the road, killing Sal's mother.

12. IAREPLEFC = 12. FIREPLACE
    Sal's father uncovered one when he learned Sal's mother wasn't coming home.

13. EHPEOB = 13. PHOEBE
    Sal entertained her grandparents with stories about her.

14. IUOXS = 14. SIOUX
    The Black Hills are sacred to them.

15. EBD = 15. BED
    "This ain't our marriage ___, but it will do."

16. LTHUIFAF =16. FAITHFUL

Gram always wanted to see Old ___.

17. SLUOJNAR =17. JOURNALS

We had no idea all the trouble they were going to cause.

18. OHCRP =18. PORCH

Place where the mysterious messages were left

19. MRAONL =19. NORMAL

Maybe dying should be ___ and terrible, according to Ben.

20. PIUSTL =20. TULIPS

Sal's mother's good-bye letter says she will return before they bloom.

21. AINHMIGC =21. MICHIGAN

Gram put her feet into this lake.

22. NGDEAA =22. AGENDA

One message said, "Everyone has his own ___."

23. ADRBTHYI =23. BIRTHDAY

Sal wanted to be in Lewiston by her mother's.

24. ONS =24. SON

Mike Bickle's relationship to Mrs. Winterbottom

25. SUHR =25. RUSH

One of the whispering words Sal heard on her trip

26. PEIP =26. PIPE

It's for remembering with: peace ___

27. BEN =27. BEN

He drew a picture of Sal as a lizard-like creature with long, black hair.

28. EHECRC =28. CREECH

Author

29. CCMNSOIA =29. MOCCASIN

A water ___ bit Gram.

30. KWYIRBA =30. BIRKWAY

Mrs. Partridge's son and Mrs. Cadaver's twin brother

31. ETNO =31. NOTE

Mrs. Winterbottom leaves one for Mr. Winterbottom saying she had to go away.

149

32. IKME =32. MIKE
The Lunatic

33. ASCNLMAAA =33. SALAMANCA
Sal's whole first name

34. RAVEG =34. GRAVE
The sheriff took Sal to her mother's.

35. DJUGE =35. JUDGE
"Don't ___ a man until you've walked two moons in his moccasins."

36. CCHEIKN =36. CHICKEN
Ben gave one to Sal.

37. EPRIRDAGT =37. PARTRIDGE
Even though she is blind, she can see everything Phoebe is doing.

38. RAC =38. CAR
Sal was locked in one with her grandparents for 6 days.

39. ADEARVC =39. CADAVER
Phoebe thinks she murdered her husband.

40. PLHOSATI =40. HOSPITAL
Gram had to go there

41. SIIREACCFS =41. SACRIFICES
According to Phoebe's mother, in life you have to make some ___.

42. OHPE =42. HOPE
The only good thing in Pandora's box

43. NBIRLOTLS =43. STILLBORN
Condition of Sal's mother's baby

44. AHZZU =44. HUZZA
Gram's saying: _____ _____ (same word twice)

45. ONOMS =45. MOONS
Walk Two ___

VOCABULARY RESOURCE MATERIALS

Walk Two Moons Vocabulary Word List

No. Word	Clue/Definition
1. ACCUMULATED	Collected or gathered together
2. AMBUSH	Surprise attack from hidden assailants
3. AMNESIA	Partial or total loss of memory caused by brain injury or shock
4. ANONYMOUS	Given or written by a person whose name is unknown
5. BADGERED	Pestered
6. BERSERK	In a state of violent or destructive rage or frenzy
7. BESIEGING	Harassing
8. BETRAYED	Deceived
9. BOUNTIFUL	Plentiful
10. CABOODLE	Lot; group
11. CADAVER	Dead body
12. CANTANKEROUS	Quarrelsome
13. CAPTIVE	One taken or held prisoner
14. CAVORTED	Pranced
15. CHISEL	Hand tool with a sharp, wedged blade
16. CHOLESTEROL	White sterol found in animal fats which can cause blocked arteries
17. COLOSSAL	Huge; gigantic
18. CONSOLE	Comfort
19. CRUCIAL	Of supreme importance
20. DEFENSIVE	Feeling under attack and hence quick to justify one's actions
21. DEFIANCE	Bold resistance to authority
22. DEFYING	Challenging; daring
23. DEPRIVED	To have undergone a loss; to not have something
24. DESPAIRING	Giving up hope
25. DIABOLIC	Very wicked or cruel
26. DISSUADE	Persuade against (an action)
27. ELABORATE	Add more details
28. EMBEDDED	Set or fixed firmly
29. EXTENSIVELY	To a great degree
30. FIENDS	Persons addicted to some activity or habit
31. FRAGILE	Physically weak; delicate
32. GHASTLY	Horrible; frightful
33. GNARLED	Knotty & twisted, as in the trunk of an old tree
34. GORGES	Deep narrow passes between steep heights
35. HAIRPIN	U-shaped
36. HANKERING	Craving; yearning
37. HOLSTER	Pistol holder
38. HORRID	Causing a feeling of horror; ugly; unpleasant
39. HYPNOTIZED	Put into a trance-like condition
40. IMPULSE	An impelling force, usually from within
41. INTRIGUING	Exciting interest of curiosity
42. LEGITIMATE	Legal; proper; within the law
43. MALEVOLENT	Wishing evil or harm to others
44. MALINGER	Pretend to be ill to escape work
45. MANNA	Divine aids; spiritual sustenance
46. MIGRAINE	Intense, periodically returning headache
47. MISCELLANEOUS	Varied; mixed

Walk Two Moons Vocabulary Word List Continued

No. Word	Clue/Definition
48. MOCCASINS	Soft, heelless, leather slippers originally worn by North American Indians
49. MOURNFULLY	Sadly
50. MUESLI	Breakfast cereal like granola
51. NOBLE	Showing high moral qualities
52. OMNIPOTENT	Having unlimited power
53. OPTIMISTIC	Having the tendency to expect the best outcome
54. ORNERY	Mischievous
55. PANDEMONIUM	Wild disorder, noise, or confusion
56. PANDORA	In Greek mythology, the first mortal woman; out of curiosity she opens a box
57. PERCOLATING	Bubbling up
58. PIOUS	Having or showing religious devotion
59. PLAGUES	Epidemic diseases that are deadly
60. PREJUDGMENTS	Judgments without all the evidence
61. PROMETHEUS	Titan in Greek mythology who steals fire from heaven for the benefit of mankind
62. RASPY	Grating; easily irritated; rough
63. REASSURANCE	Restored confidence
64. RELUCTANT	Unwilling; hesitant
65. RHODODENDRON	Shrub with showy flowers of pink, white, or purple
66. RUINATION	Demise, destruction or decay
67. RUMMAGING	Searching thoroughly by moving the contents about
68. SKEPTICAL	Not easily convinced or persuaded; doubtful
69. SPARE	Refrain from troubling or worrying
70. SPIRE	Top of a pointed, tapering object or structure, as a mountain peak
71. STILLBORN	Dead when delivered from the womb
72. SULLEN	Gloomy; dismal
73. TENTATIVELY	Hesitantly
74. TREACHEROUS	Dangerously unstable
75. UNADULTERATED	Pure
76. WEANING	Adapting a young child or animal to go without something

VOCABULARY WORD SEARCH Walk Two Moons

```
V M R S V F W M T Y E N I A R G I M C T
S U O I P R H G P L B E R S E R K A A L
A R O D N A P M A L E V O L E N T L P H
Y R D S I G R T M U A M P O V B E I T D
H S A R U I R E Q F M G S R C A N N I Z
P Y P S D L M A N N A R U N I D T G V V
A I P I P E L W V R N U O E T G A E E V
N S B N R Y F E Z U O I E R S E T R G G
D K E E O E T Y N O B N N Y I R I E H Z
E E T T S T F Q I M L A A L M E V M A N
M P R A D I I I L N E T L E I D E B S F
O T A M D E E Z E M G I L V T C L E T J
N I Y I C I P G E N N O E I P A Y D L R
L C E T O A M R I D D N C S O B K D Y K
U A D I L Y V P I N D S S N E O E E G B
M L V G O J D O U V G K I E L O D D O G
A V Y E S G N A R L E D M T A D A D R H
Z M I L S E U M E T S D C X B L U Q G B
S K N R A K S Q V D E E C E O E S M E F
L H R E L U C T A N T D F X R F S D S G
Q H O L S T E R D N M O C C A S I N S M
V H O R R I D Y A M B U S H T Z D T S T
C H I S E L A Q C O N S O L E P P H G D
```

AMBUSH	DEPRIVED	IMPULSE	PANDORA
AMNESIA	DISSUADE	LEGITIMATE	PIOUS
BADGERED	ELABORATE	MALEVOLENT	PLAGUES
BERSERK	EMBEDDED	MALINGER	RASPY
BESIEGING	EXTENSIVELY	MANNA	RELUCTANT
BETRAYED	FIENDS	MIGRAINE	RUINATION
CABOODLE	FRAGILE	MISCELLANEOUS	SKEPTICAL
CADAVER	GHASTLY	MOCCASINS	SPARE
CAPTIVE	GNARLED	MOURNFULLY	SPIRE
CAVORTED	GORGES	MUESLI	SULLEN
CHISEL	HAIRPIN	NOBLE	TENTATIVELY
COLOSSAL	HOLSTER	OPTIMISTIC	
CONSOLE	HORRID	ORNERY	
DEFYING	HYPNOTIZED	PANDEMONIUM	

VOCABULARY WORD SEARCH ANSWER KEY Walk Two Moons Vocabulary

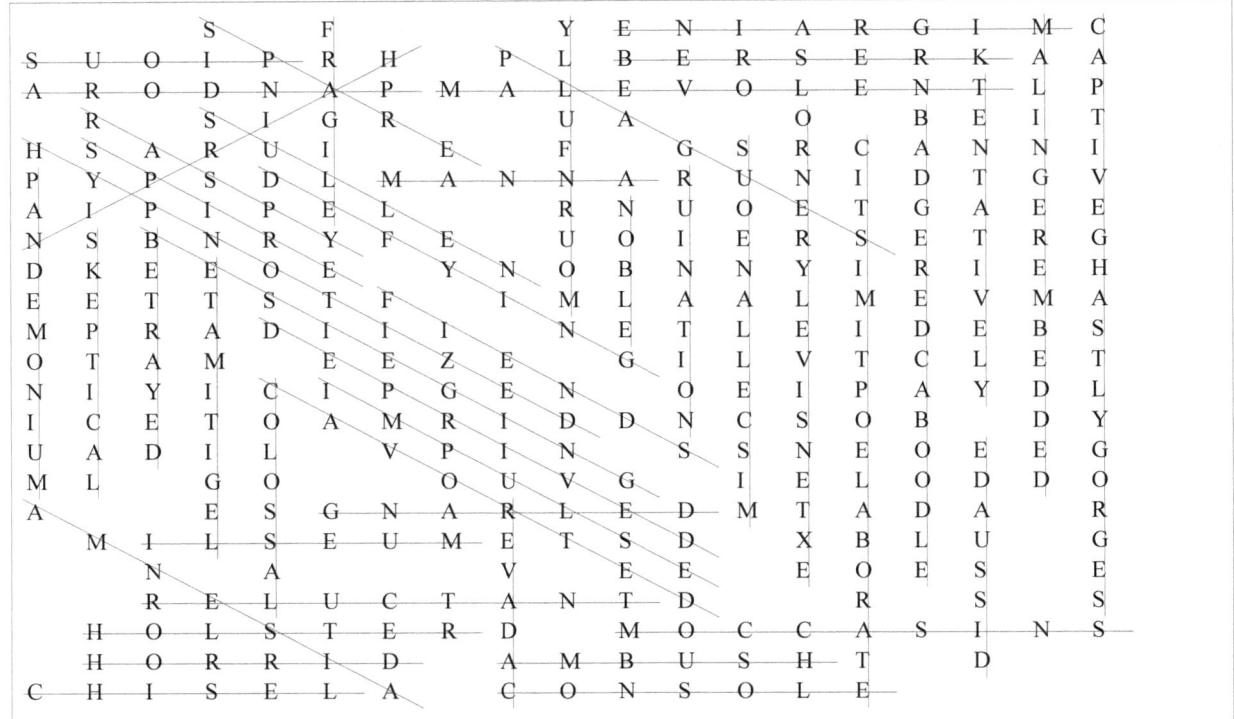

AMBUSH	DEPRIVED	IMPULSE	PANDORA
AMNESIA	DISSUADE	LEGITIMATE	PIOUS
BADGERED	ELABORATE	MALEVOLENT	PLAGUES
BERSERK	EMBEDDED	MALINGER	RASPY
BESIEGING	EXTENSIVELY	MANNA	RELUCTANT
BETRAYED	FIENDS	MIGRAINE	RUINATION
CABOODLE	FRAGILE	MISCELLANEOUS	SKEPTICAL
CADAVER	GHASTLY	MOCCASINS	SPARE
CAPTIVE	GNARLED	MOURNFULLY	SPIRE
CAVORTED	GORGES	MUESLI	SULLEN
CHISEL	HAIRPIN	NOBLE	TENTATIVELY
COLOSSAL	HOLSTER	OPTIMISTIC	
CONSOLE	HORRID	ORNERY	
DEFYING	HYPNOTIZED	PANDEMONIUM	

VOCABULARY CROSSWORD Walk Two Moons

Across
1. Deceived
5. Feeling under attack and hence quick to justify one's actions
7. Pestered
10. Surprise attack from hidden assailants
11. Divine aids; spiritual sustenance
12. Showing high moral qualities
13. Dead body
14. Collected or gathered together

Down
1. In a state of violent or destructive rage or frenzy
2. Hesitantly
3. Given or written by a person whose name is unknown
4. Add more details
6. Persons addicted to some activity or habit
8. Very wicked or cruel
9. Bold resistance to authority
10. Partial or total loss of memory caused by brain injury or shock

VOCABULARY CROSSWORD ANSWER KEY Walk Two Moons

								1 B	2 E	T	3 R	A	4 Y	E	D
		5 D	E	6 F	E	N	S	I	V	E		E		N		L
				I				E		N		O		A
7 B		8 D	G	E	R	E	9 D		S		T		N		B
		I		N			E		S		A		Y		O
		A		D			F		R		T		M		R
10 A	M	B	U	S	H		I		K		I		O		A
M		O					A				V		U		T
N		L		11 M	A	N	N	A			E		S		E
E		I					C		12 N	O	B	L	E		
S		13 C	A	D	A	V	E	R					Y		
I															
14 A	C	C	U	M	U	L	A	T	E	D					

Across
1. Deceived
5. Feeling under attack and hence quick to justify one's actions
7. Pestered
10. Surprise attack from hidden assailants
11. Divine aids; spiritual sustenance
12. Showing high moral qualities
13. Dead body
14. Collected or gathered together

Down
1. In a state of violent or destructive rage or frenzy
2. Hesitantly
3. Given or written by a person whose name is unknown
4. Add more details
6. Persons addicted to some activity or habit
8. Very wicked or cruel
9. Bold resistance to authority
10. Partial or total loss of memory caused by brain injury or shock

VOCABULARY MATCHING 1 Walk Two Moons

___ 1. LEGITIMATE   A. To a great degree

___ 2. RUMMAGING   B. Horrible; frightful

___ 3. CONSOLE   C. Persons addicted to some activity or habit

___ 4. HOLSTER   D. Legal; proper; within the law

___ 5. ELABORATE   E. Unwilling; hesitant

___ 6. OPTIMISTIC   F. Breakfast cereal like granola

___ 7. UNADULTERATED   G. Dangerously unstable

___ 8. SPARE   H. Pure

___ 9. BETRAYED   I. Not easily convinced or persuaded; doubtful

___ 10. TREACHEROUS   J. Collected or gathered together

___ 11. DEPRIVED   K. Refrain from troubling or worrying

___ 12. SULLEN   L. Demise, destruction or decay

___ 13. RELUCTANT   M. Intense, periodically returning headache

___ 14. GHASTLY   N. Persuade against (an action)

___ 15. MIGRAINE   O. Physically weak; delicate

___ 16. RUINATION   P. Mischievous

___ 17. FRAGILE   Q. To have undergone a loss; to not have something

___ 18. ACCUMULATED   R. Searching thoroughly by moving the contents about

___ 19. DISSUADE   S. Gloomy; dismal

___ 20. MALEVOLENT   T. Wishing evil or harm to others

___ 21. FIENDS   U. Having the tendency to expect the best outcome

___ 22. SKEPTICAL   V. Add more details

___ 23. MUESLI   W. Deceived

___ 24. ORNERY   X. Comfort

___ 25. EXTENSIVELY   Y. Pistol holder

VOCABULARY MATCHING 1 ANSWER KEY Walk Two Moons

D - 1. LEGITIMATE	A.	To a great degree
R - 2. RUMMAGING	B.	Horrible; frightful
X - 3. CONSOLE	C.	Persons addicted to some activity or habit
Y - 4. HOLSTER	D.	Legal; proper; within the law
V - 5. ELABORATE	E.	Unwilling; hesitant
U - 6. OPTIMISTIC	F.	Breakfast cereal like granola
H - 7. UNADULTERATED	G.	Dangerously unstable
K - 8. SPARE	H.	Pure
W 9. BETRAYED	I.	Not easily convinced or persuaded; doubtful
G -10. TREACHEROUS	J.	Collected or gathered together
Q -11. DEPRIVED	K.	Refrain from troubling or worrying
S -12. SULLEN	L.	Demise, destruction or decay
E -13. RELUCTANT	M.	Intense, periodically returning headache
B -14. GHASTLY	N.	Persuade against (an action)
M 15. MIGRAINE	O.	Physically weak; delicate
L -16. RUINATION	P.	Mischievous
O -17. FRAGILE	Q.	To have undergone a loss; to not have something
J - 18. ACCUMULATED	R.	Searching thoroughly by moving the contents about
N -19. DISSUADE	S.	Gloomy; dismal
T -20. MALEVOLENT	T.	Wishing evil or harm to others
C -21. FIENDS	U.	Having the tendency to expect the best outcome
I - 22. SKEPTICAL	V.	Add more details
F -23. MUESLI	W.	Deceived
P -24. ORNERY	X.	Comfort
A -25. EXTENSIVELY	Y.	Pistol holder

VOCABULARY MATCHING 2 Walk Two Moons

___ 1. PANDEMONIUM A. Top of a pointed, tapering object or structure, as a mountain peak
___ 2. SPARE B. Of supreme importance
___ 3. HORRID C. Knotty & twisted, as in the trunk of an old tree
___ 4. ACCUMULATED D. Causing a feeling of horror; ugly; unpleasant
___ 5. REASSURANCE E. Deep narrow passes between steep heights
___ 6. CABOODLE F. An impelling force, usually from within
___ 7. BOUNTIFUL G. Refrain from troubling or worrying
___ 8. EXTENSIVELY H. Wild disorder, noise, or confusion
___ 9. ELABORATE I. Restored confidence
___ 10. BESIEGING J. Put into a trance-like condition
___ 11. RUMMAGING K. Shrub with showy flowers of pink, white, or purple
___ 12. RHODODENDRON L. Plentiful
___ 13. ORNERY M. In Greek mythology, the first mortal woman; out of curiosity she opens a box
___ 14. SKEPTICAL N. Searching thoroughly by moving the contents about
___ 15. CAVORTED O. Pranced
___ 16. GNARLED P. Harassing
___ 17. MALINGER Q. Not easily convinced or persuaded; doubtful
___ 18. PERCOLATING R. Collected or gathered together
___ 19. CANTANKEROUS S. Bubbling up
___ 20. PANDORA T. Lot; group
___ 21. HYPNOTIZED U. To a great degree
___ 22. IMPULSE V. Add more details
___ 23. SPIRE W. Pretend to be ill to escape work
___ 24. GORGES X. Quarrelsome
___ 25. CRUCIAL Y. Mischievous

VOCABULARY MATCHING 2 ANSWER KEY Walk Two Moons

H - 1.	PANDEMONIUM	A. Top of a pointed, tapering object or structure, as a mountain peak
G - 2.	SPARE	B. Of supreme importance
D - 3.	HORRID	C. Knotty & twisted, as in the trunk of an old tree
R - 4.	ACCUMULATED	D. Causing a feeling of horror; ugly; unpleasant
I - 5.	REASSURANCE	E. Deep narrow passes between steep heights
T - 6.	CABOODLE	F. An impelling force, usually from within
L - 7.	BOUNTIFUL	G. Refrain from troubling or worrying
U - 8.	EXTENSIVELY	H. Wild disorder, noise, or confusion
V - 9.	ELABORATE	I. Restored confidence
P - 10.	BESIEGING	J. Put into a trance-like condition
N - 11.	RUMMAGING	K. Shrub with showy flowers of pink, white, or purple
K - 12.	RHODODENDRON	L. Plentiful
Y - 13.	ORNERY	M. In Greek mythology, the first mortal woman; out of curiosity she opens a box
Q - 14.	SKEPTICAL	N. Searching thoroughly by moving the contents about
O - 15.	CAVORTED	O. Pranced
C - 16.	GNARLED	P. Harassing
W 17.	MALINGER	Q. Not easily convinced or persuaded; doubtful
S - 18.	PERCOLATING	R. Collected or gathered together
X - 19.	CANTANKEROUS	S. Bubbling up
M 20.	PANDORA	T. Lot; group
J - 21.	HYPNOTIZED	U. To a great degree
F - 22.	IMPULSE	V. Add more details
A - 23.	SPIRE	W. Pretend to be ill to escape work
E - 24.	GORGES	X. Quarrelsome
B - 25.	CRUCIAL	Y. Mischievous

VOCABULARY JUGGLE LETTER 1 Walk Two Moons

1. ARCTOEVD = 1. _____
   Pranced

2. NNPOMOTTEI = 2. _____
   Having unlimited power

3. GIGNINUIRT = 3. _____
   Exciting interest or curiosity

4. EMILUS = 4. _____
   Breakfast cereal like granola

5. EYNSVELETXI = 5. _____
   To a great degree

6. SMAIENA = 6. _____
   Partial or total loss of memory caused by brain injury or shock

7. ESTKRCAUNAON = 7. _____
   Quarrelsome

8. OPSUI = 8. _____
   Having or showing religious devotion

9. HSGTYAL = 9. _____
   Horrible; frightful

10. RHRDIO = 10. _____
    Causing a feeling of horror; ugly; unpleasant

11. LTLONISRB = 11. _____
    Dead when delivered from the womb

12. EKERRBS = 12. _____
    In a state of violent or destructive rage or frenzy

13. RAEGEDBD = 13. _____
    Pestered

14. AECLDCTUUMA = 14. _____
    Collected or gathered together

VOCABULARY JUGGLE LETTER 1 ANSWER KEY Walk Two Moons

1. ARCTOEVD = 1. CAVORTED
   Pranced

2. NNPOMOTTEI = 2. OMNIPOTENT
   Having unlimited power

3. GIGNINUIRT = 3. INTRIGUING
   Exciting interest or curiosity

4. EMILUS = 4. MUESLI
   Breakfast cereal like granola

5. EYNSVELETXI = 5. EXTENSIVELY
   To a great degree

6. SMAIENA = 6. AMNESIA
   Partial or total loss of memory caused by brain injury or shock

7. ESTKRCAUNAON = 7. CANTANKEROUS
   Quarrelsome

8. OPSUI = 8. PIOUS
   Having or showing religious devotion

9. HSGTYAL = 9. GHASTLY
   Horrible; frightful

10. RHRDIO =10. HORRID
    Causing a feeling of horror; ugly; unpleasant

11. LTLONISRB =11. STILLBORN
    Dead when delivered from the womb

12. EKERRBS =12. BERSERK
    In a state of violent or destructive rage or frenzy

13. RAEGEDBD =13. BADGERED
    Pestered

14. AECLDCTUUMA =14. ACCUMULATED
    Collected or gathered together

VOCABULARY JUGGLE LETTER 2 Walk Two Moons Vocabulary

1. MIEPSLU = 1. _____
   An impelling force, usually from within

2. DVRCEAA = 2. _____
   Dead body

3. ARSPE = 3. _____
   Refrain from troubling or worrying

4. REEHAOUTRCS = 4. _____
   Dangerously unstable

5. GWAEINN = 5. _____
   Adapting a young child or animal to go without something

6. UOFBUILNT = 6. _____
   Plentiful

7. ILRGMAEN = 7. _____
   Pretend to be ill to escape work

8. SCUERAAENSR = 8. _____
   Restored confidence

9. IFGLARE = 9. _____
   Physically weak; delicate

10. SPTAEKCLI =10. _____
    Not easily convinced or persuaded; doubtful

11. IFYNDGE =11. _____
    Challenging; daring

12. SGGIEEINB =12. _____
    Harassing

13. EFDENVISE =13. _____
    Feeling under attack and hence quick to justify one's actions

14. GKHNAEINR =14. _____
    Craving; yearning

VOCABULARY JUGGLE LETTER 2 ANSWER KEY Walk Two Moons
JUGGLE WITH CLUES

1. MIEPSLU = 1. IMPULSE
   An impelling force, usually from within

2. DVRCEAA = 2. CADAVER
   Dead body

3. ARSPE = 3. SPARE
   Refrain from troubling or worrying

4. REEHAOUTRCS = 4. TREACHEROUS
   Dangerously unstable

5. GWAEINN = 5. WEANING
   Adapting a young child or animal to go without something

6. UOFBUILNT = 6. BOUNTIFUL
   Plentiful

7. ILRGMAEN = 7. MALINGER
   Pretend to be ill to escape work

8. SCUERAAENSR = 8. REASSURANCE
   Restored confidence

9. IFGLARE = 9. FRAGILE
   Physically weak; delicate

10. SPTAEKCLI = 10. SKEPTICAL
    Not easily convinced or persuaded; doubtful

11. IFYNDGE = 11. DEFYING
    Challenging; daring

12. SGGIEEINB = 12. BESIEGING
    Harassing

13. EFDENVISE = 13. DEFENSIVE
    Feeling under attack and hence quick to justify one's actions

14. GKHNAEINR = 14. HANKERING
    Craving; yearning